"Written by a diverse group of authors from various races, genders, and denominations, this book masterfully blends theory and practice, offering invaluable insights for enriching both sermon preparation and worship. With its intra-dynamic approach, this work serves as an indispensable resource for preachers seeking to elevate their ministry and engage visually and sensitively attuned congregations with creativity and depth."

—NAMJOONG KIM, Associate Dean of Doctoral Programs and International Relations for Korea, Claremont School of Theology

"This book sparks the preacher's imagination! Each contributor brings Yang's profound homiletical insights from *Arts and Preaching* to life in this compelling companion volume. Readers will be inspired to set the book down and dive into the sermon worksheets themselves, exploring more aesthetically vibrant and imaginative possibilities for preaching in the twenty-first century."

—CASEY SIGMON, Director, Pause/Play Center for Preachers, Saint Paul School of Theology

"This book is wonderful and necessary for all preachers (and listeners) who sense the need for living a truly humane and more beautiful life. These authors all sense the need for both the 'and' in 'Arts and Preaching,' as well as the hidden-but-profound 'as' in 'Preaching as Art.' The much-needed exploration of the shared core between the arts and preaching comes here to the fore."

—MARTIN LAUBSCHER, Senior Lecturer in Homiletics and Liturgics, University of the Free State, Bloemfontein, South Africa

"This helpful handbook serves as a bridge between Sunggu Yang's earlier theoretical work, *Arts and Preaching: An Aesthetic Homiletic for the Twenty-First Century*, and the everyday practice of preaching. It provides fresh insights and practical resources for preachers seeking to deepen their aesthetic approach to homiletics, offering guidance on how to move beyond familiar patterns and habitual preaching styles."

—TONE STANGELAND KAUFMAN, Professor of Practical Theology, MF Norwegian School of Theology, Religion and Society

Arts and Preaching

Arts and Preaching

A Handbook for Practice, Volume 1

Edited by
SUNGGU A. YANG

Contributors
Mónica Ibarra, Rob O'Lynn, Hyun Ho (Peter) Park, Chris Murphy, Eliana Ah-Rum Ku

CASCADE *Books* • Eugene, Oregon

ARTS AND PREACHING
A Handbook for Practice, Volume 1

Copyright © 2025 Wipf and Stock Publishers. All rights reserved. Except for brief quotations in critical publications or reviews, no part of this book may be reproduced in any manner without prior written permission from the publisher. Write: Permissions, Wipf and Stock Publishers, 199 W. 8th Ave., Suite 3, Eugene, OR 97401.

Cascade Books
An Imprint of Wipf and Stock Publishers
199 W. 8th Ave., Suite 3
Eugene, OR 97401

www.wipfandstock.com

PAPERBACK ISBN: 979-8-3852-0033-7
HARDCOVER ISBN: 979-8-3852-0034-4
EBOOK ISBN: 979-8-3852-0035-1

Cataloguing-in-Publication data:

Names: Yang, Sunggu, editor.

Title: Arts and preaching : a handbook for practice, volume 1 / edited by Sunggu A. Yang.

Description: Eugene, OR : Cascade Books, 2025 | Includes bibliographical references and index.

Identifiers: ISBN 979-8-3852-0033-7 (paperback) | ISBN 979-8-3852-0034-4 (hardcover) | ISBN 979-8-3852-0035-1 (ebook)

Subjects: LCSH: Preaching. | Arts and religion.

Classification: BV4211.2 .A77 2025 (paperback) | BV4211.2 .A77 (ebook)

05/26/25

THE HOLY BIBLE, NEW INTERNATIONAL VERSION®, NIV® Copyright © 1973, 1978, 1984, 2011 by Biblica, Inc.® Used by permission. All rights reserved worldwide.

Holy Bible, New Living Translation, copyright © 1996, 2004, 2015 by Tyndale House Foundation. Used by permission of Tyndale House Publishers, Inc., Carol Stream, Illinois 60188. All rights reserved.

New American Standard Bible®, Copyright © 1960, 1971, 1977, 1995, 2020 by The Lockman Foundation. All rights reserved

mysterium tremendum et fascinans
—Rudolf Otto

Contents

Prologue		ix
Contributors		xv
1	Painting (Cubism) & Preaching Mónica Ibarra	1
2	Architecture & Preaching Hyun Ho (Peter) Park	19
3	Fashion & Preaching Eliana Ah-Rum Ku	36
4	Film & Preaching Chris Murphy	57
5	Theater & Preaching Rob O'Lynn	76
Epilogue		95
Bibliography		97

Prologue

OVERVIEW

This handbook project began with the following core question: In our highly sensory and interactive age, how might preaching draw upon various arts to expand the aesthetic experience and mode of preaching?

    The project director, Yang, and the pastoral writing team have recognized that contemporary congregants—especially millennials—are intensely aesthetically oriented, visually and aurally aware, body focused, and holistically educated about the Bible and life itself. This multi-intelligently informed epistemological context of the audience calls for a significant paradigm shift in preaching practices. With this awareness, the pastoral team and I were committed to producing a practical pastoral handbook for the practice of artistic holistic preaching.

ECCLESIAL CIRCUMSTANCES

Contemporary preaching ought to evolve to resonate with today's spiritually hungry yet digitally and aesthetically savvy generations who find themselves estranged from church traditions. The evidence from research and pastoral insights points to a shortfall in the conventional sermon format: a sole reliance on text that fails to engage listeners seeking a more immersive, sensory encounter with their faith. The congregations of today desire a dynamic engagement with the divine message—one that appeals to all senses and fosters personal growth in multiple dimensions. As cultural trends lean toward the visual, artistic, and a celebration of the corporeal, so too must sermons adapt, integrating these elements into a holistic expression of worship.

The fusion of art and sermon holds promise for bridging this gap. Rudolf Otto highlighted art's capacity to facilitate and manifest the sacred encounter with what he termed "the numinous." Art can bring the abstract concept of the divine into the tangible realm, stimulating our senses and connecting with us on a primal level. Echoing this sentiment, Dostoyevsky saw art not as a passive vessel but as a force with the potential to enact change in the world. This view is reinforced by J. W. De Gruchy, who contended that aesthetics is indispensable for the redemptive work of the divine. These perspectives collectively endorse a blending of the artistic with the homiletic for a richer, more meaningful religious practice.

This handbook initiative aims to reawaken an appreciation for the *mysterium*, again a term coined by Otto to describe the profound and enthralling nature of the divine. This aspect becomes vital when the profundity of faith is diminished by superficial interpretations. The guide developed through the handbook endeavors to support preachers in invoking this profound awe and charm within their ministry and broader church life, utilizing artful preaching as a catalyst for change.

The act of standing in reverential silence during Handel's "Hallelujah" choruses reflects this shared understanding of *mysterium*. This instinctive reaction is rooted in Scripture and the portrayal of Jesus—the narrative core of Christianity, suggesting that the Bible itself necessitates an interpretive lens that is inherently artistic. Edward Farley's insights into art's ability to evoke a sense of the transcendent align with this project's ambition to imbue preaching with such an artistic sensibility, aiming to guide congregations toward their own transcendent experiences. In an era of fleeting attention and instant gratification, there is a risk that religious engagement becomes superficial. Yet, the enduring teachings of Christianity recognize a deeper, transformative power in the divine presence—a power synonymous with the *mysterium* that the faithful are called to experience and embrace. It is the sincere aspiration of the handbook's authors to facilitate such encounters.

The need for innovative methods is what has driven the creation of this handbook—a resource envisioned to make artistic preaching accessible to a wider audience. It is with great satisfaction that we now share the outcomes of this endeavor with the pastoral community.

CONTENT: WHAT'S UNIQUE?

In this handbook, we advocate for the practice of artistic-holistic preaching, a concept realized through meticulous intersectional research between various modern art forms (specifically, painting, film, architecture, fashion, and theater/drama) and homiletic theories. What sets this work apart from previous discussions on arts and preaching is its intra-dynamic hermeneutical approach, as opposed to merely illustrative or integrative methods. For example, when addressing the intersection of painting and preaching (a topic covered in our handbook), a preacher may reference Picasso's cubist work as a simple verbal illustration in a sermon or even display a piece of Picasso's cubist painting on a digital screen as an integral part of the sermon. However, our proposed intra-dynamic approach delves deeper, aiming to craft a sermon that is intrinsically cubist in its structure and delivery, without necessarily mentioning Picasso's name or displaying his work—because the sermon itself embodies cubism. Similarly, with architecture and preaching, the preaching experience can be inherently architectural without referencing specific buildings or architects or showing clips of aesthetic architecture.

This artistic intra-dynamic approach seeks to revolutionize our current text-heavy, minimally aesthetic homiletic education and practice. The ultimate aim of this innovative approach to preaching is to fulfill two specific needs within the church: (1) the dynamic spiritual formation of the preacher, and (2) a holistic-aesthetic and multisensory exposition and engagement with Holy Scripture by both the preacher and the congregation.

This handbook therefore is poised to enhance public worship by enriching the artistic preaching and worship experience of congregations. Artistic preaching has the potential to create a synergistic effect with other elements of worship. Given that the Bible abounds with artistic references, it is indeed a sacred task for preachers to bring the holy arts of the Bible to life, thus fostering a more vibrant and spirited congregational life.

POSSIBLE CHALLENGES

The central topic of arts and preaching can be both inclusive and exclusive to practicing preachers. Firstly, it can be very inclusive as the act of preaching is a form of well-designed and well-thought-out oral and bodily performance, which means that the practice of preaching itself can be considered a religious form of performative art. Furthermore, Christian Scripture itself is replete with artistic or aesthetic expressions such as poetry, dance, architecture, imagery, songs, fashion, and crafts, not to mention Jesus' own sophisticated storytelling. Preachers deliver their messages based on these highly aesthetic passages (although there are highly prosaic ones, like in the book of Romans). In this respect, the intersection of arts and preaching is not—and should not be—a foreign concept to any preacher. The association of preaching with the arts is fundamentally a regular part of their vocation. Thus, the topic can be very inclusive for preachers.

At the same time, however, the same topic can be quite exclusive for many preachers in various ways. To begin with, some may believe they lack artistic talents, thus perceiving the idea of artistic preaching as alien to them. Secondly, most are trained to read, interpret, and preach Scripture primarily in a historical-critical manner, not necessarily through a holistic-artistic lens. Thirdly, and particularly within Protestant church education, overall seminary instruction—which includes biblical, historical, ethical, and constructive theological studies—often lacks sufficient engagement with theological aesthetics and its valuable contributions to theological and spiritual formation. For these and other reasons, the subject of arts and preaching might seem daunting or specialized to some.

Hence, the handbook authors, who naturally find the central topic friendly and inclusive, remained acutely aware throughout the project of those preachers who might feel largely excluded from discussions about it. The team diligently sought ways to engage those who are indifferent, inviting them into the discourse and actual practice of artistic preaching through their writing and workshop planning. Fundamentally, the authors assume that all practicing preachers are supportive of the central topic and are interested in its practice. Yet, there are many who might think otherwise for valid and convincing reasons. In response to such objections and apathy, the writers endeavor to create a dialectical space in each chapter for a deeper understanding and practical engagement with the central topic.

FINAL REMARKS

This handbook is a conversion of editor Yang's 2021 theoretical book, *Arts and Preaching: An Aesthetic Homiletic for the Twenty-First Century*. Since its publication, multiple pastoral journal reviewers and general readers have expressed a desire to see the practical application of the theoretical ideas found within. Therefore, this handbook endeavors to be as practical as possible while still retaining the essential theoretical underpinnings, subtly interwoven behind the scenes, with hands-on, "how-to" approaches introduced in each chapter. Like Yang's previous book, the handbook specifically deals with the following five art forms: architecture, film, fashion, theater/drama, and painting. Music is not included, as the topic has already been discussed in a highly practical and applicable manner in Yang's earlier work.

All five authors, each responsible for a chapter, are local preachers or preaching professors who actively preach. As such, they understand well the challenges they discuss in their contributions. This also means that they are not professional artists trained in the aforementioned art forms. This might seem like a caveat, as there is a possibility that they may not present or utilize each art form effectively in a homiletical context. However, this very circumstance is a significant advantage, especially for the handbook's target audience: the everyday preacher. A core philosophy of the handbook is that any preacher, not necessarily professionally trained in the arts (though such training would be a bonus), can excel at artistic preaching with a genuine interest in the subject. The handbook's writers embody this philosophy sincerely and faithfully.

The pastoral and practical orientation of the handbook ensures that it can be seamlessly integrated into a variety of preaching courses—whether introductory or advanced. It should also be a valuable addition to the required or recommended reading lists for many DMin programs or non/denominational pastoral gatherings, especially those focused on excellence in preaching practice. For those leading pastoral gatherings, it is advisable to visit the handbook's companion website, The Center for Arts and Preaching (https://www.preachingcenter.org/), for additional resources and workshop opportunities.

As mentioned, only five specific art forms are utilized in this handbook. Indeed, numerous other art forms could have been included in this work (or Yang's original volume). Therefore, we aspire to develop a volume 2 or 3 in the future, following the publication of this handbook, and we are excited to see how the Spirit will guide this endeavor.

Finally, we extend our profound gratitude to the Calvin Institute of Christian Worship (CICW) and its exceptional director, Dr. John D. Witvliet. This handbook project would not have been feasible without the Institute's enormous support, including its generous grant program. It is our hope that this handbook will serve as a valuable resource for the Institute in its continued outstanding work in Christian worship and preaching.

Contributors

Mónica Ibarra: Assistant Director of Youth and Their Families, Village Church, Beaverton, Oregon

Dr. Eliana Ah-Rum Ku: Assistant Professor of Preaching, Graduate School of Practical Theology, South Korea

Dr. Chris Murphy: Senior Pastor, Newberg First Presbyterian Church, Newberg, Oregon

Dr. Rob O'Lynn: Associate Professor of Preaching and Ministry, Director of Graduate Bible Programs, Dean of Distance Education, Kentucky Christian University

Dr. Hyun Ho Peter Park: Senior Pastor, First United Methodist Church of Yuba City, California

Dr. Sunggu A. Yang: Associate Professor of Theology and Christian Ministries, George Fox University

1

Painting (Cubism) & Preaching

Mónica Ibarra

INTRODUCTION

What if there was a way for us as preachers to practice an art form that uniquely beholds the glory of God in the process? So often, we, as preachers of God's word, work tirelessly to exegete the divine Scriptures week after week, expending our energy to prayerfully consider what the Spirit is trying to speak through us. In our Western society, the pressure is on to have most of the answers (if not all), especially as preachers. Therefore, sometimes studying Scripture may feel more like preparing to defend your dissertation than like the divine gift God called you to. Whether this is your experience or not, it is important to acknowledge that, as pastors who preach on a weekly basis or any sort of frequency, it can be alarmingly easy to see Scripture primarily as a book to study rather than to first behold its sacredness. Before anything else, the Word of God is holy and demands to be revered. Consequently, what if there was a way for us to rediscover the innate beauty of God's word by changing the way we study and teach it?

Any day of the week for me may look and feel like chaos. I am usually running out of my house to make it on time to my first meeting of the day. Afterward, I quickly make my way back to my office with a brand new list of things to do, trying to get a head start on at least one of my responsibilities. Throughout the course of my day I have different meetings and events to attend and, as pastors, there are always spontaneous messages or calls from people that we love and shepherd. Due to the wide range of responsibilities, I feel hectic as I am constantly being pulled from one thing to the other. However, when I get home, I notice that things really came together in the course of my day. By the end of the week, there will be a complete picture of all the things I was working on with some loose ends and projects that won't be done for a few weeks or people I'm waiting to hear back from and so forth. Even in the incompleteness, God makes it all come together in perfect unity, fulfilling beautiful things in the course of my days and leaving others to be fulfilled in God's own timing. Therefore, though it may seem chaotic and lacking in order, there is actually much structure and an intentional flow. However, it may not look the way I think it should and in the end only some of what I wanted to accomplish may get done. In the end, I am not the one that makes all things come together. With all of this comes a beautiful complexity that allows us to remain in wonder. What I've just explained is our key to artistic preaching that beholds the glory of God and the divine word. That being said, let's start with a brief introduction and history to the artistic method.

SUMMARY OF ART FORM

The art form I am applying to preaching is called *cubism*. Before exploring the theology and homiletical application of the cubist approach, we must first examine the original art form from which my preaching strategy is derived. If you've read Yang's previous book,[1] you may already be familiar with some of this information. However, if you have not, I will provide a brief overview of cubism below.

At the start of the twentieth century, cubist artists craved a holistic art form which could reflect the holistic human experience. For this reason, artists were drawn to phenomenology, which can be defined as the investigation of lived experience of human beings. According to their understanding, there was no way that human beings could ever be apart from the world they lived in. Yet, somehow through Cartesian philosophy,[2] the conventional arts had created a divide between the world and its inhabitants by developing "objective" or "objectively" observable flat images that were fixed in time and space. Cubist artists, such as Picasso, saw this as a limitation of what could be.

---

1. Yang, *Arts and Preaching*, 21–26.
2. "An attempt to attain objective-rationalistic knowledge of the world by a subject who has successfully detached her- or himself from the surrounding material or affective environment" (Yang, *Arts and Preaching*, 22).

Yang makes note of cubist philosophy as following, "Thus, [in cubism] lived holistic experience of the world or the external object claims priority over distanced rationalistic-scientific observance of it. Accordingly, multi-perspectival knowledge is preferred over that of a single fixed perspective because now human eyes are not considered mere analytic lenses examining a neutral world, but lively interpreters of the ever-changing multivalent world."[3] This cubist approach had a direct impact on creative art processes. Below is an example of a flat, strictly fixed painting (Ap. Luke, AD 386)[4] compared to a multiperspectival cubist painting (Picasso, 2022).[5] Notice the difference in depth, angles, and lifelike depiction.

In the fifteenth century, many European artists had begun the exploration of three-dimensional perspectives as an artistic technique in an attempt to create an illusion of space.[6] The idea was that through the creative use of perspective as well as light and dark tones, the arts could portray an image that made the viewer feel as though they were in the art piece themselves. It would be as if the viewer was looking through the frame, at the actual object displayed in the picture. However, this was once again another conflicting idea for cubist artists. They felt that this artistic technique was deceitful and did not give a true sense of what the art pieces portrayed.

3. Yang, *Arts and Preaching*, 23.

4. https://www.pexels.com/photo/byzantine-style-fresco-of-saint-mary-in-sumela-monastery-turkey-18577782/.

5. https://pixabay.com/illustrations/pablo-picasso-two-girls-reading-7123310/.

6. "All About Cubism."

Cubist artists desired to present people, places, and objects accurately, in order to give a holistic understanding of what was being shown. Using geometric shapes, they aimed to expose diverse angles, sides, and points of view that would give the viewers a true experience of the art they were perceiving.[7] As Yang notes, for cubists, time and space are seen as constantly fluctuating, fluid elements. Therefore, their art must also resemble the realistic flow of that which we exist in.[8] In short, "Cubism is not actually interested in capturing all dimensions or the entirety of the subject. Rather, by opening up the possibility of overlapping time and space, it admits the possibility of transcendence penetrating the observed, which is not readily observable or detectable by human physicality."[9]

THEOLOGICAL AND SPIRITUAL CONNECTIONS BETWEEN CUBISM AND PREACHING

Reflecting on our own existence and the wonders of creation that surround us should make it glaringly obvious that the God we serve is art itself. The intricacies and complexities of our being are key indicators that God cannot be restrained by words and study. God has woven Godself in all things to make Godself known through it all. A leading factor that is inspiring about cubism and preaching style is that, before anything else, God is the art piece. Just like an art display, God is first meant to be admired and revered. If we were to go to a museum and see Picasso's work on one of the walls, our first reaction would likely be to walk toward it and admire what we see from a respectful distance. Then, as we observed, we would see different angles, techniques, and messages that would give us a more holistic perception of the piece. We first come before God, full of wonder, curiosity, and awe. As we spend more time with God through Scripture, prayer, and people, we obtain a more holistic view of the God we serve. Therefore, when applying the cubistic approach to preaching, we seek to reflect different perspectives and knowledge of the world, humankind, and the Triune God, as a means to gaining a more complete understanding of the—always floating, not fixed—complexity of it all.

When we read Scripture, we are reminded that God is far too great for us to fully comprehend. Psalm 145:3 sings, "Great is the Lord and greatly to be praised; his greatness is unsearchable," which is precisely a core representation of cubist spirituality. As Yang notes, in cubism "one cannot have

---

7. "All About Cubism."
8. Yang, *Arts and Preaching*, 24.
9. Yang, *Arts and Preaching*, 25.

complete knowledge of the observed"[10] because time and space are relative to the eye of the beholder, which undergoes constant change. Therefore, we are simply collecting different pieces of the whole we are pursuing. Personally, serving in a multicultural community has visually shown me that the body of Christ is much like a kaleidoscope. We are all diverse lenses with unique angles, shapes, and colors that display the image of God in a special way. However, it is only possible to create such a colorful and mesmerizing picture when we are all together showing our light, color, shape, and size, not only as individual pieces but as intersecting instruments. We come together so that the image displayed in the end is one collective reflection we are all a part of. All of God's creation has an important role in this beautiful kaleidoscope that we call church and that is to reflect, as one body, a more holistic picture of who God is.

View Through Kaleidoscope[11]

The very idea and application of transcendence is what relates cubism to Christian theology. As we examine cubist art methods exhibiting transcendence, we run into five potential principles previously addressed in Yang's *Arts and Preaching* book.[12] One especially noteworthy is the process of deconstruction and reconstruction, which takes the observed object and removes the seemingly fixed or false perception of it. The beauty of

---

10. Yang, *Arts and Preaching*, 23.
11. https://www.pexels.com/photo/round-red-and-gray-art-design-2486904/.
12. Yang, *Arts and Preaching*, 25.

this process is that it is presenting the viewer the opportunity to see the object with fresh eyes and a renewed perspective. The goal is not to deform or destroy the observed but rather to expose it in its truest form to reveal deep internal insights. Unlike destructive deconstruction processes, this one carries hope, as it deconstructs solely to reconstruct into a more holistic and liberating form. With this understanding, we can draw parallels between cubism and Christian theology. Living a cruciform life is a constant process of deconstructing ourselves in order to reconstruct into the new life God calls us to. A process in which we allow God to overcome us and transform (deconstruct) us into the beings God created us to be (reconstruct), that we may come to the realization that our incompleteness is made whole through God.

In a seminar I attended, Dr. Esau McCaulley said something that I believe truly encapsulates the whole reason for Yang's *Arts and Preaching* book. Speaking to a room full of pastors, ministers, and preachers, McCaulley said, "You are creating and adding beauty to the world."[13] I believe this is the core of who we are and the purpose behind what we do. Isn't it so beautiful that it comes down to something so simple yet so powerful? By closely communing with the Creator and the created world, we are creating and adding beauty to the world, and that is all that is required of us. Therefore, as you engage with the cubist homiletic, keep coming back to this foundational value. Let it remind you that persevering through uncertainty and incompleteness—which hereafter we will call a cubist homiletic or cubist preaching—allows space for God to speak and move in unimaginably divine ways with all innate divine beauty.

INTRA-DYNAMIC ARTISTIC METHOD OF CUBIST PREACHING

Cubist preaching allows for a diverse, wide array of possibilities when it comes to structuring and planning your sermon. As Yang notes, in the process of cubistic deconstruction and reconstruction the object can then be seen from many different angles and perspectives (e.g., inside-out, outside-in, above and below, front and behind, etc.). In the same way, the process of writing and creating the sermon can vary in more ways than we can ever imagine. Below, I present several creative methods for practicing cubist preaching, which I hope will serve as a gateway for readers to develop further innovations.

---

13. McCaulley, "Christian Imagination."

1. Co-Preaching and Teaching (*communal approach*): This method alone can be done in multiple ways, but one way that I have seen it unknowingly explored was in my own church community. Our church has an eight o'clock and a ten o'clock morning service, and often the preacher that speaks at the eight o'clock will also speak at the ten o'clock. However, every now and then, we have two different preachers for the services speaking on the same passage. This allows the two individual pastors to indirectly collaborate to present two messages to different congregations, with some crossover. Certainly, this method delivers unique messages—plural!—on the same passage. I would consider this a cubistic preaching spin-off because within cubism, the idea is that it would be the same group of people receiving different perspectives at once. Therefore, to truly apply a "communal" approach, I would encourage collaborating directly with a team of preachers in your community to co-write, co-plan, and co-study. This process would likely take a significantly longer amount of time as each preacher comes with their own perspective and interpretation. However, that's the beauty of cubistic preaching—the positive complexity of a thing explored together!

2. Perspective Analysis (*observational method*): In this method, the preacher deliberately guides the congregation through the diverse perspectives of individuals in the narrative or passage. An important detail in this process is to remember that the goal of cubistic preaching is not to give a complete picture of all perspectives but rather simply present multiperspectival insights. Yang reinforces this by drawing a parallel between cubism and Scripture, saying, "Scripture helps us to see many facets or dimensions of God, but never all of them."[14] Throughout this preaching method it is crucial to provide thorough, and even positively provocative, guiding questions as the preacher portrays each perspective. Though there will be no main or explicit sermon point presented in cubist preaching, there still needs to be some structure as the preacher guides the congregation to reflect on the word. Therefore, despite the liberating construct of this method, there are two things that we should prepare for; the first is asking good guiding questions and the second is providing historical or cultural context of the passage as needed.

   This process may look different for each congregation. However, it might be worthwhile as a common practice to create some quiet space in between the stories and perspectives. The listeners might sit

---

14. Yang, *Arts and Preaching*, 29.

with their thoughts or do an activity to help guide them through the message and Scripture, especially if they are used to receiving fully fledged sermons with clear answers and points. A helpful way to think through this method is to allow these three questions to be foundational for the overall message. First, what does the passage mean for them in their context? Second, what does the passage mean for the preacher today? Finally, what does this mean for the life of the world? A potential creative element the preacher could use in this preaching method is to have a loop of a cubist painting being created on a screen while preaching, following the sermon section by section. The preacher could also have a live painter portraying their interpretation to help stir the minds of those in the congregation as they hear the message and see it visually crafted.

3. Storytelling Scripture (*narrative focused*): While the previous two methods incorporate elements of storytelling, Storytelling Scripture is distinct in that it fully immerses the congregation within the narrative itself. Rather than using a story as a tool to illustrate a theological point or reinforce a predetermined message, this approach allows the story to be the message, unfolding organically through multiple perspectives. Cubist preaching naturally aligns with storytelling, as it seeks to make sense of Scripture through fragmented yet interconnected viewpoints, much like how cubist art presents multiple angles within a single composition. This approach moves away from rigid interpretations, inviting both preacher and listener to engage actively and experientially with the passage. As Sunggu Yang notes, a cubist preacher is both a communicative and creative agent—not merely delivering a sermon but participating in its unfolding reality alongside the listener. Yang describes this preacher as one who is "both in charge of the matrix generation and also participates in the matrix along with the listener."[15] In this way, the preacher is not just a storyteller but a co-navigator, discovering meaning in real time alongside the congregation. This method transforms preaching into an interactive process, where meaning is not imposed from a single authoritative voice but rather emerges through a collaborative and dynamic engagement with Scripture. Storytelling Scripture, therefore, does not seek to resolve a narrative into a singular takeaway; instead, it invites ongoing exploration, interpretation, and participation in the biblical story itself. In this section, I would like to draw emphasis on Indigenous theology, since Native American culture has a deeply rooted identity in their

---

15. Yang, *Arts and Preaching*, 35.

storytelling. Rev. Dr. Randy S. Woodley draws comparisons between the Western worldview and Indigenous theology, revealing that Native Americans generally "understand truth through narrative and instinctively find" their place in the story "and activate toward that truth."[16] In Indigenous theology and culture, most of their teaching and preaching is done through the medium of storytelling. However, Woodley observes that Western culture is short on stories: "The story in the Western world is the thing you tell as the concluding point, or the children's moment in some traditions."[17] He mentions that "Indigenous worldviews might say that we understand narrative has truth, and facts are, well, not so important as truth."[18] This means that stories may more often be used as a filler or complementary piece in Western culture rather than seen as carrying powerful truths. According to Woodley, about "90 percent of the Scriptures are narrative."[19] Therefore, the way that we understand and value narratives and storytelling will change and impact the way we read Scripture.

Now, regarding the cubist preaching methodology in general, it is important for preachers to amplify the significance of storytelling not only for themselves but also for those in our congregations whom we serve. There's a possibility that we can be missing people because we are so fact driven, needing all the details in order to feel that we've given a well-formatted sermon. However, it is safe to say that God's word does not need our validated facts in order to be validated itself. This being said, there are endless ways to deliver a message through storytelling, especially if we are retelling the gospel story. Much like the previous section, we would need to ask good guiding questions and provide necessary context but also set the scene for the congregation to feel *in* the story. This does not mean that we would have to stick to story passages in Scripture nor do we have to stick to the exact biblical storytelling format. Rather, we can add creative elements in our preaching, such as incorporating a palindrome poem—a storytelling technique that can be read forward and backward. We can use live theatrical exposition of Scripture that can bring the story to life (see chapter 5, "Theater & Preaching," for more details), and so forth. The point is to emphasize the importance of the story as a narrative that holds powerful truth, which God shared with his creation that we might find him in the midst of it all.

16. Woodley, *Indigenous Theology*, 61.
17. Woodley, *Indigenous Theology*, 48.
18. Woodley, *Indigenous Theology*, 47.
19. Woodley, *Indigenous Theology*, 47.

I would like to add that the three methods listed above are inspired by Yang's own cubist sermon composition[20] but have been slightly altered to reflect my own alteration. In the sample sermon provided in his *Arts and Preaching*,[21] I propose some blend of methods two and three, Perspective Analysis and Storytelling, while maintaining his nine rules of sermon composition. Regardless of the method one chooses to apply in cubist preaching, the goal is the same, namely, to display "the immanence and transcendence of the Divine entangled in the fabric of the universe."[22] The cubistic preaching method is not meant to be a greater challenge for us as preachers but rather to free us from the hermeneutical box we live in in order to explore our God-given creativity more freely. From planning our sermons all the way to our delivery, the cubist approach to preaching should inspire awe and wonder of our Creator or *mysterium tremendum et fascinans* of the Divine as Otto puts it. It should allow us to live out the beautiful words of Scripture that we speak over others' lives and apply them to our own lives—glaringly being aware that there is so much more we cannot know or understand. In that way, we may find beauty and encouragement in all things that God brings together, no matter how seemingly incomplete and chaotic the process may be.

---

20. Yang, *Arts and Preaching*, 37.
21. Yang, *Arts and Preaching*, 39.
22. Yang, *Arts and Preaching*, 28.

SERMON PLANNING WORKSHEET

Note: This is a general guide. Depending on the homiletic approach, the preparation process may need to be adjusted.

Scripture:	Initial Thoughts or Feelings:

First Impression of Awe, Wonder, or Curiosity:

Multifaceted Listening:

Preaching Method:	Evaluate Nine Rules:

Framework:

Scripture: LUKE 10:30-37

Initial Thoughts or Feelings: How could they ignore a man half-dead? Cruelty... Accustomed? What was different about the last man? Such deep, sincere goodness

First Impression of Awe, Wonder, or Curiosity: The Samaritan reflects Jesus' heart through his behavior. What compelled him to modify his journey for the stranger? Soothing his wounds was already good but he gave so much more!

Multifaceted Listening:

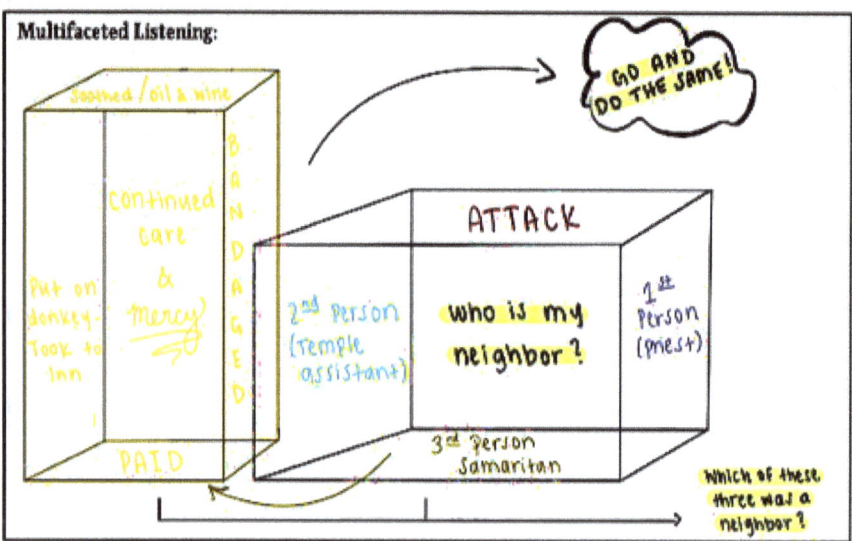

Preaching Method: Perspective Analysis

Evaluate Nine Rules: Paragraph form, no key idea, no concrete flow (start to end), open structure, invitational language, cohesive conclusion

Framework: Yang's paragraph format, open questions > invitational > conversational > thought-provoking > story overview > perspective evaluation (1st impression) > historical context > cultural context > invitational Q's > encounter text 2nd time > imaginative listening > reflection > biblical context > application invitation > final reflection and personal conclusion

SAMPLE SERMON

In this homily, I've used the structure provided by Yang in his sample sermon, dividing it paragraph by paragraph and referring to each section as a "piece." The cubistic preaching method being used is the Perspective Analysis rooted in some of the nine rules addressed by Yang.[23]

> Luke 10:30–37 (New Living Translation)
> Jesus replied with a story: "A Jewish man was traveling from Jerusalem down to Jericho, and he was attacked by bandits. They stripped him of his clothes, beat him up, and left him half dead beside the road. By chance a priest came along. But when he saw the man lying there, he crossed to the other side of the road and passed him by. A Temple assistant walked over and looked at him lying there, but he also passed by on the other side. Then a despised Samaritan came along, and when he saw the man, he felt compassion for him. Going over to him, the Samaritan soothed his wounds with olive oil and wine and bandaged them. Then he put the man on his own donkey and took him to an inn, where he took care of him. The next day he handed the innkeeper two silver coins, telling him, 'Take care of this man. If his bill runs higher than this, I'll pay you the next time I'm here.' Now which of these three would you say was a neighbor to the man who was attacked by bandits?" Jesus asked. The man replied, "The one who showed him mercy." Then Jesus said, "Yes, now go and do the same."

Piece 1

Upon our first reading of this Scripture passage today I'm curious to know, what stands out to you at first glance? Take a moment to think or maybe write some things down that caught your attention [*pause—individual reflection*]. Now that you've gathered your own thoughts, turn to the person(s) next to you and share your first impressions with one another [*pause—communal reflection*]. When we've heard a story so many times, it can be difficult to hear it again and find your own perspective in the story without immediately getting drawn back to what we've learned about this passage in the past. At first glance, the beating given to the Jewish man may seem ugly, cruel, animal-like, at least it is to me. My initial reaction to the first and second bystanders is shock, surprise, especially since one man is a priest and the other is a temple assistant. My negative shock toward these

---

23. Yang, *Arts and Preaching*, 37.

men then gradually shifts to a positive surprise as the story continues and we encounter the Samaritan and observe his actions. What was the need for this story? Why do you think it is so specific? What was Jesus teaching through this parable?

Piece 2

I'm sure many of us have heard this story from different perspectives, maybe even different perspectives of those in the story. For example, like thinking through what could've gone through the minds of the temple assistant and the priest that made them not want to stop and help. When hearing this story, how have we seen ourselves in it? Who do you relate to the most? Many of us are probably very hesitant to compare ourselves to the religious leaders and instead say we would probably be most like the Samaritan. But is that really true? As churchgoers and followers of Christ of course we don't want to fall in the category of those that didn't act as neighbors to a person in need. In today's world, where might we have already fulfilled some of these roles in different ways? Who might we have already walked past that would have benefited from our service and neighborly conduct? Who might we have hurt? Or maybe you've come here today feeling a lot like the battered man lying half-dead.

Piece 3

Looking at this specific story in the context and time period it was written, there are many things for us to notice. In the verses prior to this passage we see that Jesus is sharing this parable with an expert of Jewish law who was asking Jesus, "How can I inherit eternal life?" Jesus had responded by letting the expert in law answer, and he said, "By loving God in soul, mind, and strength and loving your neighbor as yourself." Jesus affirmed but the religious leader asked again, "But who is my neighbor?" and so Jesus begins the parable of the Samaritan. When Jesus tells parables throughout the Gospels, we know it's not random and, although many times he's not giving clear answers and is sometimes purposefully confusing, he is nothing short of intentional.

Jesus started the story with a Jewish man, someone the expert of the law could relate to, and then he introduced two others, the priest and the temple assistant, who again, the expert of the law could connect with. However, for religious leaders it was basic Jewish law that you should help those in need. We see to what extent this law was in place in Exodus 23:5, which says, "If you see the donkey of someone who hates you fallen down under its load, do not leave it there; be sure you help them with it." Therefore, even the animals of people they didn't get along with should be cared for. How do you think the expert of the law interpreted this part of the story? Could he have been shocked that the priest and temple assistant passed the Jewish man by? After all, he was Jewish. The people with religious duties knew the law, had it memorized, and were first to enforce it, so why might they have neglected their duty, and why would Jesus portray them this way?

The last person to be introduced in the story is the Samaritan; for us this might just seem like a random person in the story but, again, Jesus is intentional. Historically, Jews and Samaritans became enemies after Assyria (today's West Asia) conquered northern Israel and the two groups had intermarriages. There was a crossover of culture through ethnicity but also through religion; however, it was neither a fully Jewish nor non-Jewish religion. Therefore this created tension between the two groups; Jews saw themselves as superior to the Samaritans, who were a mix of Jewish and Assyrian blood, practicing half-pagan religion. Samaritans were outcasts. So it's interesting that Jesus chooses a Samaritan to be not only mentioned in the parable that he's telling to a Jewish religious leader but to be the one who sets a good example of what it means to be a neighbor. How do you think you would feel being the religious leader hearing this story?

Piece 4

I'm going to invite you to step into the story now as we re-read the passage again this time from a different translation (NASB). You can close your eyes if it helps, you can jot down notes or draw, or do something else to help you use your creative imagination. Set the scene and find yourself in the story. Pay attention to what feelings arise as you listen; what do the people look like? What about those passing by, what are their reactions like? What else is going on around them? Okay, let's read the story again:

> Jesus replied and said, "A man was going down from Jerusalem to Jericho, and he encountered robbers, and they stripped him and beat him, and went away leaving him half dead. And by coincidence a priest was going down on that road, and when he saw him, he passed by on the other side. Likewise a Levite also, when he came to the place and saw him, passed by on the other side. But a Samaritan who was on a journey came upon him; and when he saw him, he felt compassion, and came to him and bandaged up his wounds, pouring oil and wine on them; and he

put him on his own animal, and brought him to an inn and took care of him. On the next day he took out two denarii and gave them to the innkeeper and said, 'Take care of him; and whatever more you spend, when I return, I will repay you.' Which of these three do you think proved to be a neighbor to the man who fell into the robbers' hands?" And he said, "The one who showed compassion to him." Then Jesus said to him, "Go and do the same."

Stay in the story and take a moment to process what thoughts and feelings came up along with the things you noticed. Write down some of those key observations. What new insights do you now have about this story? When picturing Jesus telling this story to the religious leader, do you have an idea as to what he was trying to communicate and why? Write it down.

Piece 5

Josh Porter, who is an author, musician, and pastor, wrote for the Bible Project an article about the parables of Jesus. In the article, "Why Did Jesus Speak in Parables," he poses this thought: "Jesus is concerned with the power of creative imagery, symbolism, and beauty, and we should be too. He wants his audience to do more than listen and think; he wants them to imagine and feel, to be challenged and provoked."[24] Tim Mackie and Jon Collins, creatives on the Bible Project team, also realize that the parables meant "to explain how he was bringing the Kingdom of God."[25] So as we look at this parable of the Samaritan, what does this reveal about the bigger picture of the kingdom of God? One thing is clear: Jesus was teaching the expert of the law what it should look like to be a good neighbor, and according to the parable, being a good neighbor is not limited to the people who are easy to love. Throughout the Gospels, Jesus was constantly pushing the boundaries of the teachers of the law and many others; just the mere fact that he was calling himself the Messiah but riding in on a donkey was a big statement about the (different) kingdom of God (Luke 19:28–40). Now what does his teaching through this parable mean possibly for us in our context today? Which of our own boundaries might he be challenging?

---

24. Porter, "Why Did Jesus Speak," para. 23.
25. Mackie and Collins, "Decoding the Gospels."

Piece 6

The Gospel of Luke is traditionally attributed to Luke, a historian, physician, and disciple of Jesus, as one of the earliest accounts of Jesus' life and ministry. In his writing, Luke is intentional about emphasizing that God's kingdom is upside-down, in essence; he does this by highlighting how Jesus welcomes all people, especially those seen as "the least," and overturns power structures. Therefore, the story of the Samaritan is no exception to Luke's literary style. With this in mind, we can assume that Jesus' parables are far too complex to be reduced to a single meaning. However, knowing the intentionality behind them we can also move forward with caution to not overemphasize or overdissect pieces of the story that were not part of Jesus' message in the first place. So, looking at the parable of the Samaritan, what have you heard God speak to you today? Take a few moments to reflect as you need [*pause*] [*prayer conclusion*].

Notes

The full sermon example was meant to follow a loose structure, not necessarily having a fixed beginning or end, as Yang suggested through the nine rules, with the exception of the last question. Nonetheless, the loose structure is not without guidance. As previously mentioned in the Perspective Analysis method, it is important to ask a significant amount of provocative questions to help keep the listener engaged but also actively participating, not simply a passive hearer. Another important part of this structure is providing the historical and cultural context of the given passage. Since we are not preaching a main point or idea, we provide significantly less information than we usually do during typical preaching. There are many benefits to this, but it can also feel to the listeners like we're leading them nowhere. For this reason, guiding questions alongside an appropriate amount of the relevant context will be crucial to ensure that the listener has the resources necessary to draw their own informed conclusions. Of course, we're also trusting that God is speaking to our listeners in unique ways. After all, cubist preaching is a warm invitation to lean into Scripture and the Spirit of God, and the listener will go as far as they accept the invitation.

CONCLUSION

The artistic method of cubistic preaching is breaking through Western worldviews, in a space and time when information is extremely accessible and over-glorified. It is an encouragement for the church to reimagine and to be challenged and transformed by hearing cubist God, if you will, revealed in Scripture. It is an invitation to think beyond a one-liner answer, a quick fix, or a three-step "how to" on spirituality and have deeper relationship with the divine. What if nothing but a sliver of God was revealed in the sermon we heard last Sunday, yet two or three more slivers are revealed when we pause to sit in wonder? I wonder if the things that would reveal God to us the most are the very things we do the least. Perhaps that's why we desperately rummage through information, as if that would be enough.

I am hopeful that we, as preachers, can better utilize the gift of having many of God's people gathered in one space to listen. Hopefully, we can also better relay the importance of communal living, including the reading and discernment of Scripture. Cubist preaching is just the beginning—helping all of God's people become comfortable with asking more questions than receiving answers, finding God in awe and curiosity, and embracing the multifaceted, unexplainable beauty of our Creator.

May we find freedom in many ways within this preaching style. May it cultivate in us an even greater desire to worship, and may it fill our souls as we return to the basics—simply creating the framework for the art piece that is none other than God's own self. In the words of one of my favorite preachers, "May his resurrection presence continue to be demonstrated and witnessed through how we live today and for the rest of our lives." Amen.

2

Architecture & Preaching

Hyun Ho (Peter) Park

INTRODUCTION

Worship space creates both inspiration and complaint. "With the organ and the beautiful stained-glass windows . . . it just almost makes me cry. It is so wonderful," said a former parishioner of mine after coming out of the pandemic and back to in-person worship in the main sanctuary. On the contrary, my effort to create a more modern-theater-looking contemporary worship space with black curtains and stage lighting in the Fellowship Hall caused more backlashes than intended splashes. I was confronted, "Isn't God light, not darkness?" and "Where are symbols of Christian faith?" I brought a cross and put it on an altar table for worship next Sunday. Another member said to me about his spiritual experience not in a church building but in the woods, "I was walking in Armstrong Redwoods State Natural Reserve. I felt like I was being one with God." Whether it is awe, annoyance, or amalgamation, space does more than what meets the eye.

Space tells a story.[1] Since Christian ministry—worship, fellowship, and discipleship—is about *how to tell* the story of God's salvation in Jesus Christ, the architecture of a building or place deserves or even, I venture to say, demands our attention. From the creation in Genesis to the building of the tabernacle in Exodus and ultimately to the restoration of Jerusalem in

---

1. Yang, *Arts and Preaching*, 48n9.

Revelation, God is not only a storyteller but also an architect and builder (Heb 11:10).[2] It is the same with preachers. With the mastery of words, their job is to make *space*—whether it is a worship place or a vision of ministry—alive and align the stories in the Bible with the lives of people. I am compelled to say, therefore, that *architecture is a means of aesthetical contemplation, theological exploration, and spiritual formation.* It is precisely the goal of this chapter to showcase that.

The main text to which I will apply architectural analysis and aspirations is Genesis 2:8–17 and 3:22–24 in which the garden of Eden is laid out and soon after Adam and Eve are laid off. Although the proposed text does not contain a physical building, it has a *blueprint* of the garden, *gan* (גן)—a fenced enclosure.[3] The main architecture on which I will focus is the sanctuary of the First United Methodist Church of Santa Rosa, where I used to serve. This choice is intentional since readers will find more similarities than differences *between* my former church's architectural underpinnings and theological implications *and* those of their own worship spaces.

This chapter first introduces how architecture can be a useful art form for preaching from a conceptual and philosophical point of view. The discussion moves to how to choose certain texts and architecture for preaching. The essay then applies five principles of an architectural hermeneutic Sunggu Yang illustrates in his book to the chosen text from Genesis with a worksheet at the end. Lastly, the sample sermon illustrates how this new hermeneutic can evoke the sense of aesthetics—awe and wonder—and ultimately invoke the transcendent.

THE RELEVANCE OF ART FORM TO PREACHING

Surely, there is no simple answer, especially for preachers who feel so far removed from this particular discipline or not so inclined to art as a whole, including myself. Yet, here is good news any preacher will be delighted in.

First, "*Architecture is communication.* Architecture tells stories."[4] My initial story with parishioners captures such a crucial characteristic of architecture. Stained-glass windows depicting the life of Jesus are meant to instill

---

2. In the same vein, an artist, Makoto Fujimura, writes, "The Bible begins in Creation and ends in New Creation. . . . God is an artist." Fujimura, *Art and Faith*, 150.

3. Yang suggests the following passages of scripture for architectural preaching: Gen 11:4, 6:14–16; Deut 22:8; Josh 8:31; 1 Kgs 6:1–10; 2 Chr 3:1–17; Ezra 3:7–13; Neh 3; Ps 118:22; Prov 24:3–4; Isa 54:11–12; Jer 22:13–14; Ezek 42:1–20, 43:10–17; Matt 21:42; Luke 6:48–49; 1 Cor 3:10–13; Eph 2:19–22; Heb 11:10; and Rev 21:9–22.

4. Yang, *Arts and Preaching*, 47 (emphasis original).

the story of Jesus, just as Gothic cathedrals stir one's "yearning for eternity" and thus convey the ultimate values of life.[5]

Second, *architecture creates a beauty*. I agree with Louis Sullivan's dictum "Form ever follows function."[6] Yet functionality, even formality, should not ever trump the fundamental drive and motive of art itself—the pursuit of beauty. Although the basics of architecture like space, form, person-environment interaction, materiality, and structure of the building are to be considered in its architectural design,[7] a building without beauty is like an unsharpened pencil. It has no point. Denis R. McNamara says, therefore, "A *beautiful* church is the very image of heaven itself made known in material form."[8] Evoking the sense of aesthetics is the beginning of architectural communication and where preaching and architecture intersect and are intertwined.

Third, *architecture is a medium of interaction*. Yang points out two spiritual elements of architecture: "first, its practical and multidimensional experience of the Divine, and second, the Divine's active interaction with nature and humanity at large."[9] Stained-glass windows are *inside* the church sanctuary not just for aesthetic contemplation but for episodic admonition and spiritual transformation. A church steeple with a cross at the top surrounded by trees and houses *outside* evokes a sense of awe and wonder and, at the same time, the presence of the Divine amid human success, struggles, and sadness. When walking *inside* the building, sometimes we feel a need or want to pray or even kneel. Is this spatial, emotional, divine, or humane? I think it is all of them.

Fourth, *architecture is a conveyor of the ultimate values*. Architecture in a nutshell is "what architects design," particularly designing "inhabitable space."[10] Since humans are the focal point of architecture, any consideration in architectural design, such as "movement, enclosure, center, periphery, geometry, structure, and signs," is geared toward enhancing the people's lived experience or, as Jaime Roberts puts it, "human needs, human circumstances, and human value systems."[11] National Memorial for Peace and Justice in Montgomery, a.k.a. the National Lynching Memorial, which Yang

---

5. Yang, *Arts and Preaching*, 48.

6. Sullivan, "Tall Office Building," 409, cited by Yang, *Arts and Preaching*, 55.

7. For a brief introduction to architecture watch Roberts Architecture, "What Is Architecture?"

8. McNamara, *Catholic Church Architecture*, 3 (emphasis added), cited by Yang, *Arts and Preaching*, 54.

9. Yang, *Art and Preaching*, 55.

10. Roberts Architecture, "What Is Architecture?," 00:34–00:44.

11. Roberts Architecture, "What Is Architecture?" 01:52–01:58.

showcases in his book, is an excellent example. Those who visit are invited not only to the horror of lynching but also to the power of healing.[12] In this sense, I concur with Yang, who says, "Architecture as an art form and spiritual practice has salvific power."[13]

In sum, architecture is a means of communication, beauty, interaction, and aspiration. Juxtaposed side by side with preaching, we are struck by their similarities despite the different mediums they employ—woods, bricks, steel, cement, and glasses over words, gesture, change of tone, and use of media, to mention a few. When these two somewhat distant disciplines come together, they can create not only art but also aesthetic wonder.

CHOOSING TEXT AND ARCHITECTURE

The first step toward an architectural hermeneutic is to select a passage that incorporates architectural elements such as buildings, structures, or blueprints. For preachers following specific texts like the Revised Common Lectionary or preaching through sermon series, this approach may not be used every time they stand in the pulpit.[14] However, it presents an opportunity for artistic exploration, exegetical wrestling, and hermeneutical innovation whenever a relevant text is chosen.[15] Sample texts recommended by Yang include Noah's ark (Gen 6:14–16), the tabernacle (Exod 26:1–6), Solomon's temple (1 Chr 3:1–4), and the new Jerusalem (Rev 21:22–27).[16]

However, the choice should not be limited to obvious passages. Preachers are encouraged to think creatively and select texts that can inspire architectural imagination in their listeners. For instance, the creation story in Genesis 1 can evoke the image of God as the master-builder who appreciates symmetry, interdependence, and productivity. Similarly, the parable of the prodigal son (or father) in Luke 15 illustrates another aspect of God as the father who restores his household—*oikos*—by actively engaging with

---

12. I highly recommend you to watch Michael Murphy's powerful TED talk, "Architecture That's Built to Heal."

13. Yang, *Arts and Preaching*, 56.

14. Thomas Long introduces four different ways to select a sermon text in his book *Witness of Preaching*, 71–73: (1) *lectio continua*; (2) a lectionary; (3) local plan; (4) preacher's choice.

15. Just as with any method of preaching, an architectural hermeneutic begins with a study of the text: "To *hear* in that text a specific word *for us*." Long, *Witness of Preaching*, 69 (emphasis added). It is no surprise that in his monumental work, Thomas Long first picks up in the third chapter, "Biblical Exegesis for Preaching," after laying theoretical foundations on preaching in two previous chapters.

16. Yang, *Arts and Preaching*, 45–46.

and rebuilding relationships—between himself and his younger son, his older son, and ultimately between the two sons.[17]

Once the text is chosen and a preliminary reading is complete, the next step is to select an architecture.[18] Preachers have several options to consider.

1) *Popular buildings.* Listeners can easily imagine themselves in these settings, as they may have visited or seen them before. These buildings can range from sacred sites like the Sistine Chapel in the Vatican and Notre Dame de Paris, to secular tourist destinations like the Lincoln Memorial in Washington, DC, or Sydney's Opera House. The building doesn't need to be globally renowned; preachers may also choose local sites that parishioners are familiar with, such as a local museum or historic building.[19]

2) *Intimate buildings.* Preaching is inherently context specific, and so should be the choice of architecture. When every listener has been to or regularly visits a particular building, a sermon can become more personal, relevant, and enjoyable. This is why a preacher's local sanctuary can be an excellent option. Local church buildings and sanctuaries often embody theological and artistic beauty, with profound symbolism in their structure. Why look elsewhere when you have such a treasure close at hand? I will explore this further later in this essay.

3) *Attractive buildings.* It is also perfectly acceptable for preachers to introduce listeners to a new architectural structure they have visited.[20] Since the building may be unfamiliar to most, if not all, attendees, they may be captivated by its beauty and design. Preachers can enhance engagement by displaying images or even giving a virtual tour of the building on screen. Acting as a guide, the preacher can lead the congregation step-by-step from entrance to exit, intertwining this exploration with the text being discussed, keeping the congregation engaged and intrigued.

I think this stage of architectural preaching is like a matchmaking. You have a sense that two *can* be a good match. As they get to know one another, they will find out who they are and how they can fit each other. If they are not meant to be, a wedding is not going to happen. If they are meant to be,

---

17. Park, "Parable of the Prodigal Son."

18. At this point of sermon preparation, understanding the structure and the main message of the text is necessary.

19. As a former Santa Rosa resident, I may choose, for example, the Charles M. Schultz Museum, better known to locals as the Snoopy Museum or Old Courthouse, in downtown Santa Rosa.

20. For me, Emory University's Cannon Chapel in Atlanta, Georgia, which is Paul Rudolph's architectural genius, or Yonsei University's Luce Chapel in Seoul, South Korea, with its unique architectural design, come to mind.

the rest will be history. In the end, just like marriage, its goal is to mutually enhance the beauty and mystery of the text and the building.

APPLYING AN ARCHITECTURAL HERMENEUTIC

The next step for preachers is to engage their architectural senses and imagination. Similar to sermon preparation, an architectural hermeneutic begins with exegesis—carefully analyzing the text and its preaching context, and bridging the gap between them.[21] After wrestling with exegetical inquiries, preachers are encouraged to sit and engage in perhaps the most critical part of sermon preparation: doing nothing. Allow the word to come to you. Become one with the text until you feel as though you are walking within it. This is akin to what Rudolf Otto describes as *mysterium tremendum*, an encounter with the holy amid mystery.[22] Immerse yourself in the narrative until it becomes vivid and real, evoking goosebumps and a chilling, trembling feeling down your spine, much like Isaiah's cry, "Woe is me!" (Isa 6:5) and Peter's plea, "Go away from me, Lord, for I am a sinful man!'" (Luke 5:8). Do not begin writing until this experience occurs. Let the word of the Lord come to you first. Only then will you understand why you must preach and who you are as a preacher.[23]

After this experience, preachers put on their architect's glasses and begin to outline an initial sketch. Yang's five principles, as laid out in his book, are particularly helpful at this stage.[24] I will add one more principle to the list at the end.

1. Multidimensional-spatial exploration of the text: *Identify* a building or structure. What are the basic spatial units of the text? Does it have an entrance and/or exit? Where is (are) the center(s)? For example, the new Jerusalem in Revelation 21 sits on a high mountain with three gates on each of four walls radiating the glory of God from everywhere.

2. Aesthetic-transcendental exploration of the text: *Intensify* the awe and wonder of the building. What artistic details does the building have?

---

21. I suggest five Ws and one H of biblical exegesis. (1) *Where* does a specific unit of the text begin and end? (2) *What* is the historical and literary context of the text? (3) *Who* are the main characters? Or *what* are the central objects? (4) *Why* is there a movement or transformation taking place in the text? Preachers also need to consider the following questions beyond exegetical endeavor. (5) *When* is this sermon preached? (6) *How* can the message of the ancient text be relevant to listeners' lives today?

22. Otto, *Idea of the Holy*, 12–40.

23. Yang, *Arts and Preaching*, 8–16.

24. Yang, *Arts and Preaching*, 56–63.

What is mysterious or even majestic about the building to you? What provokes transcendental wonder when you gaze upon it?

3. Performative-interactional exploration of the text: *Imagine* a walk-through and your reaction. How would you respond if you walked there? For example, surrounded by seraphs and their cry of "Holy," would you say the same, "Awe to me," like Isaiah if you were in the temple and seeing a vision of God (Isa 6)?

4. Exploration of oppositional or binary dimensions of the text: *Establish* structural symmetry or oppositions. Are there any structures going hand in hand? Is one structure a counterpart of the other?

5. Eco-interactional exploration of the text: *Explore* ecological interactions. Are there living creatures or God's creations? If so, do they interact with one another? How do their interactions amplify the other four aforementioned explorations of the text?

6. Intertextual exploration of the text: *Evoke* scriptural references. Have you seen a building or structure like this somewhere else in the Bible? Are there any words or images that intensify their connections? What are the theological claims that undergird such repetition and construction?

While intriguing and enlightening, not every text lends itself to applying all five (or six) principles. Forcing a text into these categories can lead to a hermeneutical red herring and an exegetical disaster. It is essential to focus on what is clearly evident in the text. Clarity should always take precedence over confusion in preaching, as in any human endeavor. Preachers may also incorporate additional explorations as they see fit.

DETERMINING THE SERMON FORM

The text and the architecture are decided. Preachers have looked at the text with multiple glasses. They know what to say, at least the gist of it. Now is the time to figure out *how* to say it. Determining the form of preaching is so critical that Thomas Long said, "Form is as important to the flow and direction of a sermon as are the banks of a river to the movement of its currents."[25] Since architectural preaching evokes and centers around images, most sermon forms focusing on the internal logic of the text and its application from the sermon's introduction to the conclusion do not fit.[26] They are so one-dimensional and rationally oriented that they often lack

---

25. Long, *Witness of Preaching*, 117.
26. For various forms of preaching, see Allen, *Patterns of Preaching*.

space for aesthetic contemplation.[27] New wine calls for fresh wineskins. So does an architectural homiletic.

Which form do preachers choose? (1) *Pictorial Sermon*. Preachers may use vivid preaching, just as Alyce M. McKenzie proposes, to today's visual listeners. For example, she breaks down a sermon into multiple meaning blocks and the sermon progresses as scenes keep changing.[28] When applied, "sermon flow is not literary-linear, but rather pictorial-episodic."[29] (2) *Episodic Sermon*. The constant movements back and forth between text and architecture divide a sermon into multiple sections. As the sermon moves from the entrance of the building to its exit, preachers may add an anecdote or two in between different segments to make the transition smooth and keep listeners engaged. (3) *Aesthetic Sermon*. Much like Eugene Lowry's *Homiletical Plot*, preachers may begin a sermon by proposing "ambiguity" of both the text and the architecture of their choice and move toward a "resolution" as the sermon progresses to the end and reveals what is at the center of the building.[30] The goal is, however, not just "experiencing the gospel" but being astounded by the beauty and mystery of God's presence.

WRITING AN ARCHITECTURAL SERMON

Now, let us get to work.

1) *Choice of the text*. I have chosen the garden of Eden story in Genesis 2:8–17 and 3:22–24. It neither is a lectionary text as a whole nor contains a physical building. Genesis 2:15–17 and 3:1–7 are the Old Testament readings for the first Sunday in Lent (Year A). Yet, the chosen text is part of the lectionary reading, elucidates a physical structure, the garden, and contains a plot—a paradise is given and lost. At the same time, "cherubim" at the end reminded me of the ark of covenant and made me wonder, "What's going on here?" So, pay attention to the details and be ready to be surprised.

> And the Lord God planted a garden in Eden, in the east; and there he put the man whom he had formed. Out of the ground the Lord God made to grow every tree that is pleasant to the sight and good for food, the tree of life also in the midst of the garden, and the tree of the knowledge of good and evil.

27. Allen, *Contemporary Biblical Interpretation*, 108.
28. McKenzie, *Making a Scene*, 25–26.
29. Yang, *Arts and Preaching*, 63.
30. Lowry, *Homiletical Plot*, 12: "A sermon is a plot. . . . Something is 'up in the air'—an issue not resolved . . . resolve matters in the light of the gospel and in the presence of the people."

A river flows out of Eden to water the garden, and from there it divides and becomes four branches. The name of the first is Pishon; it is the one that flows around the whole land of Havilah, where there is gold; and the gold of that land is good; bdellium and onyx stone are there. The name of the second river is Gihon; it is the one that flows around the whole land of Cush. The name of the third river is Tigris, which flows east of Assyria. And the fourth river is the Euphrates.

The Lord God took the man and put him in the garden of Eden to till it and keep it. And the Lord God commanded the man, "You may freely eat of every tree of the garden; but of the tree of the knowledge of good and evil you shall not eat, for in the day that you eat of it you shall die." (vv. 8–17)

Then the Lord God said, "See, the man has become like one of us, knowing good and evil; and now, he might reach out his hand and take also from the tree of life, and eat, and live for ever"—therefore the Lord God sent him forth from the garden of Eden, to till the ground from which he was taken. He drove out the man; and at the east of the garden of Eden he placed the cherubim, and a sword flaming and turning to guard the way to the tree of life. (vv. 22–24 NRSV)

2) *Let the word come to you.* After a preliminary exegesis,[31] I have pictured myself over and over again in the garden surrounded by trees full of

---

31. I have tried to answer the five Ws and one H of the biblical exegesis I proposed earlier. (1) *Where does a specific unit of the text begin and end?* The text begins with the creation of the garden and ends with its closure. (2) *What is the historical and literary context of the text?* It is part of another, if not the second, account of Creation in Gen 2:4b–25 and of the fall in Gen 3:1–24. Here, the pinnacle of God's creation is not the creation of humans unlike the first Creation story in Gen 1:1–2:4a, but the creation of the Garden. (3) *Who are the main characters?* The main characters are the man—אָדָם: *adam*—God the busy architect, and cherubim at the end. *What are the central objects?* The text highlights the garden. Even the reason why Adam and Eve are brought into the garden is to "work"—עָבַד—there and to "watch/keep"—שָׁמַר—it (Gen 2:15). At the heart of the garden is the Tree of Life as well as the Tree of Knowledge of Good and Evil. The garden is closed for humans not to have access to the Tree of Life. (4) *Why is there a movement or transformation taking place in the text?* The man along with his wife eats the forbidden fruit from the Tree of Knowledge of Good and Evil and is kicked out. The garden is permanently closed down. (5) *When is this sermon preached?* I aim to deliver the sermon on the first Sunday of Lent following the Lectionary. What does entering the passion of and with Jesus have to do with entering and exiting the garden? Can we return to the garden? If so, how? (6) *How can the message of the ancient text be relevant to listeners' lives today?* I have asked myself, "What paradise God has placed me here and now?" "Where have I been fallen from the grace of God?" "What would God's

fresh fruits, streams of water flowing through, and gold and precious stones everywhere. Suddenly, I felt like singing, "Better is one day in your courts than a thousand elsewhere."[32] I couldn't be happier. Then, something happened. Light has gone. Darkness came. I found myself driven away. With my hands covering my head, I shouted, "What have I done?" I ran, turned around and saw the gate was shut. I wondered, "Can I ever go back?"

3) *Choice of the architecture.* I have chosen the sanctuary of the First United Methodist Church of Santa Rosa where I used to pastor and worship. Though not widely known, it was an intimate and attractive space for me and my weekly listeners. The sermon can be a holistic and participatory experience inviting the audience to use all the senses available to them—hearing, sight, smell, and touch. It will be a visually rich experience since the sanctuary is surrounded by stained glass windows depicting the life of Jesus from his birth, death, and resurrection to his ascension.[33] Furthermore, it has a red carpet in the middle leading to the narthex area with three entrances. Two podiums on each side are elevated above the ground. The altar with a cross on it is placed at the center of the red carpet. This sanctuary coincides with the layout of the garden of Eden. Just as a river flows (from a center?) and creates four streams, the red carpet visualizes such a movement. The front-right pulpit where a preacher delivers a sermon stands up like the Tree of Knowledge of Good and Evil disseminating the word of life. Just like the Tree of Life, the altar in the middle seems to be the source of water.

4) *Analyze the text with architect's eyes.* I have focused on spatial elements of the text and made the following discoveries.[34]

1. Multidimensional-spatial exploration of the text

- Basic spatial units of the text: There are five units—(1) a garden placed in the east; (2) ground full of trees and their fruits; (3) the Tree of Knowledge of Good and Evil and the Tree of Life amid the garden; (4) a river flowing and creating three branches; (5) east of the garden with the cherubim, its (gate)keepers.

- Architectural entrance and exit points in the text: There is no entrance. However, the exit seems to be where the cherubim stand (or fly over?).

---

invitation back to the Garden look like for me and my church community?"

32. Psalm 84:10 (NIV). Matt Redman composed a song in 1995 based on Psalm 84, "Better Is One Day," which is widely sung in contemporary worship services even today.

33. For virtual tours of the stained-glass windows of the First United Methodist Church of Santa Rosa see "Altar Window"; "Clerestory Windows"; and "Round Window."

34. This section closely follows the questions and criteria Sunggu Yang proposes in Yang, *Arts and Preaching*, 60–62, except (6) Intertextual exploration of the text.

- What spatial points are at the center? The Tree of Life is at the heart, if not physically at the center, of the garden and should be guarded at all costs. The Tree of Knowledge of Good and Evil is also located in the middle of the garden.

2. Aesthetic-transcendental exploration of the text
   - Architectural details of the text: The text provides specific names of the rivers—Pishon, Gihon, Hiddekel, and Euphrates—and of the lands around them—Havilah, Cush, and Assyria. Are those names historical, literal, or symbolic? The text also reveals at the end the identity of garden keepers—cherubim. Why cherubim all of a sudden?
   - Theological or spiritual nature of the transcendental wonder provoked in the architectural composition of the text: The garden of Eden is an archetype of paradise. Trees, rivers, gold, precious stones, and the man working there are to show the glory of God's creation.

3. Performative-interactional exploration of the text
   - I imagined myself taking a walk in the garden. Like a little shepherd boy, I sang, "The Lord is my shepherd. I shall not want. He makes me lie down in green pastures. He leads me beside still waters. He restores my soul" (Ps 23:1–3a). I was dumbfounded when I got kicked out. So, what has happened? Is there a redemption?

4. Exploration of oppositional or binary dimensions of the text
   - Eden has four rivers. Why? Are they in pairs? The Tree of Life is paired with the Tree of Knowledge of Good and Evil. Are they oppositional? If not, what is their relationship with each other?

5. If any, eco-interactional exploration of the text
   - Water and soil become resources for trees and their fruits, as they also become food to man (and other creatures). The man and the woman can interact with other living creatures, as Adam gives their names (Gen 2:19–20a). Yet, what is so significant about their interaction with the serpent that made them get kicked out?

6. Intertextual exploration of the text
   - Cherubim, four-winged celestial guardian creatures, appear prominently in the creation of the tabernacle. Two cherubim face each other while turning their faces toward the mercy seat of the

ark of covenant (Exod 25:20). Between two cherubim God has spoken and delivered the words to the Israelites (Exod 25:22). Is the garden of Eden similar to the ark of covenant or the tabernacle in its structure? If so, what would living in or returning to the garden mean?

5) *Choice of the form*. I have chosen the pictorial sermon to amplify its visual effect in delivery. After introductory stories, the sermon will be divided into four sections: (1) *Center* (Zoom In)—the scene moves from the man in the middle of the garden to trees around him and ultimately the Tree of Life and the Tree of Knowledge of Good and Evil (vv. 8–9). (2) *Over* (Zoom Out)—the camera enlarges its view and focuses where four streams of river flow (vv. 10–14). (3) *Entrance* (Zoom In)—God gives an orientation to a happy camper. The sermon will mirror this sequence by journeying through the sanctuary of the First United Methodist Church of Santa Rosa. (4) *Exit* (Zoom In and Out)—God finds out the violation, expels campers, and shuts down the garden. Additionally, I will incorporate episodic and aesthetic elements, concluding with personal stories. What is the point of architectural preaching if there is no story to tell and no art and awe to be found?

SERMON PLANNING WORKSHEET

1. TEXT	Gen 2:8–17 and 3:22–24	
2. PRELIMINARY EXEGESIS	1) *Unit*	Opening and closing of the garden
	2) *Context*	In creation story
	3) *Characters and Objects*	Man, God, cherubim, and two trees
	4) *Plot*	Humans eat the forbidden fruit and are expelled
	5) *Timing*	First Sunday of Lent (Year A)
	6) *Message*	Grace is always there for those who (re)turn to God
3. ENCOUNTERING THE WORD	"It's so good to be here!" "Oh my . . ." "Can I go back?"	
4. ARCHITECTURE	Sanctuary of the First United Methodist Church of Santa Rosa	
5. ARCHITECTURAL ANALYSIS	(See above)	
6. SERMON FORM	Pictorial, episodic, and aesthetic	

SAMPLE SERMON

"Experiencing Grace and Returning to the Garden"

Note: This sermon is designed to be highly visual and aims to engage the senses of the listeners.

Have you ever been to a place where you so loved it or were so astounded that you didn't want to leave? In January 2023, my family went to Horseshoe Bend in Arizona (*image 1*). This natural beauty and mystery took my breath away. Even my six- and four-year-olds were so mesmerized that they stopped talking for a while. After spending an hour, we headed out. I asked later, "Where is mom?" Just like the holy family looking for boy Jesus, we went back and frantically looked for a seventy-year-old. I found her standing still and staring at nature's sublime. When I shouted, "Mom!" she reacted, "Oh!" as if she woke up from a dream, from awe and wonder to the ordinary.

I felt the same when I went to Berkeley Rose Garden with my wife for the first time (*image 2*). Like Adam waking up from his sleep and shouting "Woo~ Man!" as a newly married, I walked in the garden with my LOVE. Flowers were in blossom with the sound of the creek flowing in the middle. We were the only two there enjoying the beauty of creation. I didn't want to leave.

Horseshoe Bend[35]   **Berkeley Rose Garden**[36]

Neither did Adam. (*Center*: Zoom In) Imagine yourself being Adam in the garden of Eden. When you open your eyes—for the first time!—you see trees beautiful and plentiful with delicious fruits, maybe some apple trees, peach trees, lemon trees, you name it or save it for dinner. Then you turn and see a little farther two big trees, I guess, in the middle of the garden.

---

35. https://pixabay.com/photos/horseshoe-bend-grand-canyon-1908283/.
36. Photo Credit: Hyun Ho Park.

One is the tree of life and the other is the tree of the knowledge of good and evil. Just like two pillars connecting the heaven and the earth and sustaining God's temple, there they are. So are you who are made in the image of God standing, staring at God's creation, and thinking, "I don't want to leave this place. I can't and shouldn't leave."

And there is more. (*Over*: Zoom Out) You lift your eyes, see farther and there are streams of water flowing out, not just one but four!—Pishon, Gihon, Tigris, and Euphrates. You may wonder *whether* those rivers are real or *where* they are now or *if* we should take them literally or symbolically like each of them symbolizing honey, milk, balsam, and wine *or* Babylonia, Media, Greece, and Rome. Let's not dig a rabbit hole here because you're in a garden, not in a classroom.

Now, you're not just standing and doing nothing there. (*Entrance*: Zoom In) You, happy campers, are getting an orientation, as you're entering the garden. "Here it is," says a voice and gives you tools for gardening—a trowel, a shovel, a rake, and many more. By the way, does anybody like gardening? Guess what? God likes gardening too! God so loved gardening that God built the garden—it's the first thing!—right after creating the heavens and the earth and placed there Adam and Eve made in God's image not just to stare at it but to "work"—עָבַד—and "watch/keep"—שָׁמַר—it. I imagine, "Give me a shovel. I'll show you how it can be done," says Eve. "Yes, dear," says Adam and *he* follows *her*.

(*Center*: Zoom In) Let's pause here and look around this sanctuary we're in (*image 3*). What do you see in the pews? The Bible and Hymnal through which you are spiritually nourished. Lift your eyes a little farther and look at the center in the front. What do you see? You see an altar where the body of Jesus, the bread from heaven, is given to us to give us life eternal. On your right, we have one more—a podium from which the word of God is proclaimed to discern what is good and bad. Have you ever been in a worship service where you felt like it was just you and God in prayer, praise, and proclamation, and you didn't want to leave?

(*Over*: Zoom Out) Now, I invite you to look little farther (*Image 4*). Do you see a stream following from the center? It's not water but a carpet. What color is this? Red. Is it a coincidence or divine providence that our church decided to have a red carpet? I think, there should be no more dispute over the color of the carpet, at least here, because it signifies the blood of Jesus flowing from the altar where the lamb is slain and sacrificed. Like the streams in the garden of Eden, it flows from the center and diverges into multiple directions, into three in our case—one to the center, another to the west, and another to the east.

Sanctuary (*Center*)[37]   **Sanctuary (*Over*)**[38]

Just like Adam and Eve, we don't come into this sanctuary just to watch the service but to join the service. (*Entrance*: Zoom In) We're like priests entering the tabernacle in the wilderness or the temple in Jerusalem. We move from the ordinary to the holy. We eat and drink something so ordinary and experience someone so extraordinary. Whether you are preachers, acolytes, ushers, communion servers, choir members, or regular attendees, we are here to work in, build, and keep God's kingdom where *shalom* is manifest and we walk daily with God.

Let's take a moment, bring our senses back to the story, and listen to what happens to Adam and Eve, *to you* in the garden. Here comes a voice once again. "You see the trees in this garden? You can eat all of their fruits." You say, "Yes!" because who doesn't like buffet and unlimited food? "Yet," says the voice, "except the one in the middle of the garden. You see the tree of the knowledge of good and evil?" "What about it?" you ask. "When you eat of it, you will die," says the voice. "Why?" you ask, but there is no answer. So, you—a man—without a clue do what he is supposed to do. He goes and tells his wife.

And we all know what happened. (*Exit*: Zoom In and Out) A serpent deceives Eve. She eats the forbidden fruit. Adam eats it as she did. When God confronts him, he blames his wife and God, "It's the woman who made me do it! By the way, you gave her to me. I'm innocent!" Do you like this guy? I don't. He is being passive-aggressive and proving himself to be a loser. And he along with his wife is kicked out of the garden that he enjoyed so much at first. Imagine yourself again being Adam and Eve. You're wrapping your head with your hands and shouting, "What have I done? What in the world did I think? Can I ever come back?" You run toward the gate in sin

---

37. Photo Credit: Hyun Ho Park.
38. Photo Credit: Hyun Ho Park.

and shame. You turn around and see the garden and its gate. You see the gate once open is now closed and see the cherubim you didn't see at first now standing at the gate. The creature has a sword flaming and turns to guard the way to the Tree of Life. And you ask yourself, "Can I ever go back?"

Have you ever asked that question to yourself? I have. About fifteen years ago, when I was in Atlanta, I took my youth group students to a weeklong conference in Philadelphia. That summer, I was busy taking a Greek intensive course, working full-time at a Korean church, and preparing for an upcoming GRE (Graduate Recording Examinations). Balancing my studies with the spiritual needs of my students was challenging. Despite feeling unprepared, I attended the conference two weeks before the GRE with a sense of desperation.

There I heard God's voice and realized my need for God's blessing in my life. "I don't care about the score. Wherever God leads me, I will be okay. What I need first and foremost is not score but God's blessing." I came home. A week later, I took the exam and I received not only a high score but also a high energy—the outpouring of the Holy Spirit for the first time in my life. I felt like I was walking with God every day in the garden. I was talking but I knew, it was the Spirit of God speaking through me. The fire lasted for two weeks. Then, something happened. You know what happened. Sin crept in and I lost it. "What have I done? Can I ever get it back?" I wondered ever since.

Then, in January 2024, I went to a gathering of Korean pastors and joined in singing "O Come to the Altar" which I knew and sang many times in our praise team.

"Can I ever go back?" the answer to my yearning to return to the garden was right there at the altar! "You don't need to do anything but come to me. Forgiveness is already given through my sacrifice. I did everything for you. My arms are wide open. All you need to do is simply come," the voice said.

Today is the first Sunday of Lent in which we meditate upon and participate in the suffering of Jesus through fasting, prayer, and almsgiving. We join those spiritual disciplines not for the sake of suffering per se but for the sake of the saving grace God granted to us through Jesus Christ. Where do forgiveness, acceptance, and redemption take place? Right here, right now.

The idea of cherubim standing at the gate and guarding the way to the Tree of Life may seem out of place at first glance, but it's not without precedent. Where have you seen cherubim in the Bible most frequently? In the description of the ark of the covenant and, therefore, in the building of the tabernacle and later in the temple. Two cherubim face each other while turning their faces toward the mercy seat of the ark of covenant. It is between these two cherubim God speaks and delivers the words to the

Israelites, remember? In other words, the garden of Eden is a microcosm of not only the ark of covenant but also the tabernacle and the Jerusalem temple with the Holy Place and the Holy of Holies in its core.

Now, why am I telling you this? Look around. We're in the garden of Eden. Right when you enter this sanctuary, you are in the Holy Place and where I, a preacher, am standing is the Holy of Holies with the altar in the middle, with a cross symbolizing the sacrifice of our savior, Jesus Christ, the lamb of God, God incarnate, King of Heaven who came to the lowest place in a manger and died on a cross in the cruelest way possible to give sinners like you and me salvation. From this altar flows the blood, forgiveness, life, hope, and future. The gate once closed is now wide open to all who sincerely confess their sins and failures and come to the throne of God.

Isn't it amazing to look at? Isn't it astounding to think about? Isn't it a breathtaking story to meditate on and share? Can I ever go back? Can we ever go back to the garden? Is restoration ever possible? The answer is "Yes, of course!" So, come, come to the Altar! The Father's arms are open wide!

CONCLUSION

In his seminal work, *As One Without Authority*, Fred B. Craddock highlighted the wordsickness of his contemporaries, noting "the changed shape of the human sensorium as a result of television."[39] That was half a century ago. Today, young people rarely watch TV; instead, they spend more time on smartphones, tablets, or even virtual reality gear. Society is increasingly becoming visually oriented. The goal of architectural preaching, or any aesthetic hermeneutics and thus homiletics, is to awaken and develop latent neurons within the preacher that are innate but underdeveloped. As preachers activate these senses in their study of text and architecture, they stand first and foremost in awe and wonder. With newfound treasures or voices heard, they become guides to their congregation. This aesthetic beauty, as Kierkegaard described, is "*a something* which one cannot directly communicate to another."[40] Listeners need to experience it as profoundly as accepting the gospel message for the first time. Preachers can only extend an invitation. The transformation of hearts is the internal work of the Spirit. Let architectural beauty enrich the homiletical endeavor, conveying what simple utterance alone cannot achieve.

---

39. Craddock, *As One Without Authority*, 9.
40. Cited in Craddock, *Overhearing the Gospel*, 3 (emphasis added).

3

Fashion & Preaching

Eliana Ah-Rum Ku

INTRODUCTION

When we consider fashion, we might think of an unending flow of new items being swiftly replaced by even newer ones, or we might reflect on a tendency toward totalizing specific, prescribed trends, irrespective of geographical context, body shape, color, or financial standing.[1] However, if we align with Miuccia Prada, one of the world's most renowned designers, in her assertion that "Fashion is instant language,"[2] we may first contemplate the communicative dimension of fashion. But what does Prada intend when she characterizes fashion as a language? Is she suggesting, in an epistemological sense, that the language of fashion functions as a specialized code, one that only those who are versed in its grammar and vocabulary can comprehend and articulate? Must we learn the grammar of fashion, a construct that appears to continually evolve, in order to effectively communicate through it?

I have two children, who are two years apart. When they were younger, I would dress them in identical outfits from head to toe, according to my own sense of fashion, regardless of their preferences. However, one day, the older child expressed a desire for change, saying, "Mum, I only want to wear black clothes and black shoes now." Notably, the eldest, has very sensitive

---

1. Covolo, "Re-Fashioning Faith," 52.
2. Galloni, "Prada vs. Prada."

skin and is particularly concerned about the materials of the clothes she wears. Although her school requires a uniform, she received special permission to be exempt from this requirement due to her sensitivities. Even in the sweltering summer humidity, she insists on wearing thick white socks that reach up to the knees, valuing comfort over others' perceptions of beauty. For my child, given her personal situation, clothing serves primarily as a means of protection and comfort. This experience underscores the multifaceted and response-able nature of understanding the communicative aspect of fashion, as it demonstrates that even when someone may not fully grasp another's fashion choices, those choices remain a form of personal expression.

In the book *Arts and Preaching*, Yang articulates that fashion encompasses a range of meanings, including physical appearance, shape, habitual practice, and a particular lifestyle or behavior; it carries functional meanings related to physical and psychological self-protection, image-making, social protest, ritual, symbolism, and even spiritual communion with the divine.[3] Yang further contends that clothing serves as a vital medium for spiritual inspiration and communication, as well as a key instrument for social communication and identity formation.[4] How do these seemingly various aspects of fashion's communicative capacities resonate with the sense of preaching?

In this chapter, I will summarize, analyze, and expand on the key elements of fashion's resonance with preaching. Specifically, I will demonstrate the application of various strategies of "fashionista preaching" as presented by Yang in *Art and Preaching*. Finally, through a sample sermon, I will delve into how it engages with the dynamic and multifaceted interplay between fashion and preaching, where God and the participants create a deeply spiritual and aesthetically rich relationship.

THE RESONANT STYLES BETWEEN FASHION AND PREACHING

Preaching can be enhanced by scrutinizing how fashion generates and conveys messages, interacts with audiences, innovates through reflection on the zeitgeist or spirit of the times, and influences the social environment.[5]

Firstly, fashion is embodied communication. It involves the whole self, not just words. Contemporary listeners tend to trust and listen more deeply

---

3. Yang, *Arts and Preaching*, 21.
4. Yang, *Arts and Preaching*, 123.
5. Yang, *Arts and Preaching*, 123.

with someone whose entire life and being embody their message.[6] Secondly, fashion is aesthetic communication.[7] While opinions on the standard of beauty may vary, fashion can be understood as an expression of the true self—a beauty that emerges from authenticity. Even if one does not match the language of another's fashion, it is valuable as sacred material. For instance, although one might feel somewhat unacquainted with the portrayal of beauty in the Song of Songs, they can still recognize the loveliness in the speakers' gaze and language, offering an opportunity to broaden their own perspectives. Thirdly, fashion serves as a medium for civil protest, its visibility and sensibility carrying the potential for transformation. The protest embodied by fashion has reshaped how we dress, how we perceive ourselves, our societal roles, and our identities as autonomous individuals.[8] Fourthly, fashion is only complete when it is tried, interpreted, and embraced by real people. A designer does not solely contribute to the entirety of the creative process; the other part is fulfilled by those who respond. In preaching, the participants engage in an "on-the-spot" interpretation, discerning the explicit and implicit truths of the design and embodying certain aspects of those truths in their own lives.[9] No single sermon fits everyone; the message is personalized through this interaction. In preaching, fashion is participatory, eschewing rigid claims of right or wrong in its attempts and interpretations. Finally, fashion transcends mere visibility and touch. It shapes perceptions, values, and ways of life, and most importantly it remains open to the unknown and the unexperienced.[10] For example, Korean aesthetics emphasize the beauty of white space, recognizing the dynamic creation that empty space generates in relation to filled space. This celebrates the unknown, the elements that may lie beyond our understanding. In the divine fashion of loving beings, this process involves encountering mysteries beyond our comprehension.

In this sense, considering the communicative aspect of fashion in preaching liberates us from the arrogance of absolute value or authoritative interpretation, opens us authentically to the incomprehensible, and thereby empowers us to engage in a creative and imaginative response-able communication.

---

6. Yang, *Arts and Preaching*, 128.
7. Yang, *Arts and Preaching*, 128.
8. Yang, *Arts and Preaching*, 129.
9. Yang, *Arts and Preaching*, 129.
10. Yang, *Arts and Preaching*, 130.

CHOOSING TEXT AND FASHION

The first step in fashionista hermeneutics involves identifying a text that contains direct or metaphorical elements of fashion and reading it through the eyes of a fashionista. While this hermeneutic approach is not universally applicable, Yang argues that a preacher fulfills a multifaceted role—perceived as "designer, maker, and showcaser"—by examining, reimagining, enhancing, and communicating the practice of preaching through the lens of fashion.[11]

As Yang suggests, preachers might envision a designer God in Genesis 3:21 or a God clothed in holy white robes in Mark 9:2–4.[12] However, even texts that make no explicit mention of clothing, such as the pericope of the woman accused of adultery (John 7:53—8:11), can be explored through a fashio-interpretive lens. When selecting a text and drawing fashio-interpretive insights, a preacher can consider several theological factors.

1) *God as a Fashion Designer.* God creates garments for Adam and Eve (Gen 3:21) and designs the priestly garments (Exod 28:3, 15–17). This divine act of dressing is extended to humanity through spiritual imputation. Humanity, created in God's image, is clothed with God's righteousness, glory, and beauty.[13] As Kuyper suggests, when he states that "there is not a square inch in the whole domain of our human existence over which Christ . . . does not cry, 'Mine,'" it may imply that God's original plan was to clothe all creation with Godself.[14]

2) *Fashion as Dual Symbolism.* In Genesis 3:21, the act of clothing is intertwined with the awareness of both human failure and divine care. This seemingly paradoxical dynamic is gospel because only when we acknowledge human impossibility do we truly appreciate divine possibility (grace).[15] Just as a flower's "naturalness" derives from its "finitude and mortality,"[16] this awareness transforms God's care into a perceived gift. Moreover, the shedding of animal blood to clothe Adam and Eve reminds us of the blood on Calvary.[17] Christ became the garment that covers the shame and imparts righteousness to those God loves.

---

11. Yang, *Arts and Preaching*, 138.
12. Yang, *Arts and Preaching*, 139.
13. Boston, *Human Nature*, 10.
14. Bratt, *Abraham Kuyper*, 461.
15. Wilson, *Four Pages*.
16. Mitchell, *Meeting Mystery*, 54.
17. Phillips, *Exploring Genesis*, 63.

3) *Fashion as Prophetic Identity.* The Bible frequently uses clothing to signify the calling and status of prophets, such as John the Baptist's camel hair garment with a leather belt (Matt 3:4).[18] While there is no uniform prophetic fashion archetype, fashion serves to reflect a distinctive prophetic identity, tailored to specific contexts and missions. It can be countercultural, challenging the status quo, subverting oppressive systems, and offering alternative visions to communities. Such challenges highlight God's enduring concern for the marginalized and oppressed, warn against false peace, and foretell the downfall of corrupt powers.[19] For prophets, wearing certain garments, like a clerical collar, can help one's thoughts and actions with religious teachings. Thus, clothing, in relation to identity, embodies the human desire to draw closer to God.[20]

4) *Fashion as Fulfillment or Restoration of the* Imago Dei. Mark's description of Jesus wearing a mystical white robe on a perfect human body (9:2–4) shows that the resurrection is both spiritual and physical.[21] This mystical robe invites us to envision the restoration of the *imago Dei* in relation to Christ (Gal 3:27; 1 Cor 15:53–54).[22] As Galatians states, those who are baptized into Christ are clothed with Christ (3:27)—God clothes us not merely with our skin, but with "God's own self."[23]

5) *Fashion as Eschatological Vision.* The book of Revelation portrays worshipers dressed in white robes, washed in the blood of the Lamb. Similarly, Ezekiel 16:8 uses clothing as a symbol of salvation within the context of an engagement ritual.[24] The Bible is replete with "fashio-aesthetic images" of the last days (cf. Dan 3, Ezek 44:17–19, Zech 8:23, Ps 45:13, Gal 3:26–27). Revelation, in particular, describes how tattoos, vehicles, hair accessories, and garments play an integral role in apocalyptic imagery (19:11–13, 16).[25]

APPLYING A FASHIONISTA HERMENEUTIC

Preachers might explore fashio-hermeneutic strategies for preaching by considering Yang's three fundamental elements of fashion: color, texture,

---

18. Yang, *Arts and Preaching*, 134.
19. Yang, *Arts and Preaching*, 135.
20. Handayani, "Does God Care," 304.
21. Yang, *Arts and Preaching*, 136.
22. Yang, *Arts and Preaching*, 136.
23. Winner, *Wearing God*, 36.
24. Handayani, "Does God Care," 301.
25. Yang, *Arts and Preaching*, 137.

and shape.²⁶ Firstly, preachers can engage in a kinesthetic or embodied interpretation of the text, involving the whole person, including both mind and body. Secondly, preachers may consider several critical inquiries: how do preachers embody "visible" communication in the biblical text through color, texture, and shape? How do these visible elements, when engaged through imagination, contribute to the creative meaning-making process of the text's words, phrases, sentences, and beyond? What connections can be established between these components? Furthermore, how can the preacher reimagine or restructure the original materials of the text through processes akin to cutting, sewing, finishing, weaving, and so on?

DESIGNING THE SERMON FORM

Theological and biblical considerations require the preacher to consider how to make communication concrete in the sermon. Yang suggests three dimensions—illustratively, integratively, and intra-dynamically.²⁷

First, the illustrative approach employs fashion as a tool to elucidate the central message. Yang draws a connection between "the fine pink linen" wrapped around a newborn child, who cries out in fear of the new world, and the scene in Genesis where God clothes Adam and Eve in garments made from skins, revealing God's love and care. Second, in the integrative approach, the metaphor of clothing or fashion becomes a key element of the message, drawing it closer to the core message. As mentioned in Ephesians 6:13–17, the imagery of "wearing" extends beyond a mere physical metaphor into the spiritual realm. This leads us to think about what it means for Godself to be our garment and our actions in wearing it—discipleship, hospitality, and testing. Third, the intra-dynamic approach, in terms of literary techniques, can be more sophisticated and the sermon itself can feel like the creation of a garment. The spiritual, physical, social, cultural, attitudinal, and visual aspects of life are all intricately woven together. This approach works through the preacher's weaving and the interaction with the participants, where each person is clothed in their own style.

These three approaches may or may not be used together within a sermon, and logical reasoning may not express a harmony or sudden entanglement of these approaches.²⁸ Fashionista preaching may seek to free up the process of preaching to open up new space and relationships with God, to penetrate the realm of the incomprehensible, to await things that

26. Yang, *Arts and Preaching*, 138–45.
27. Yang, *Arts and Preaching*, 141–45.
28. Yang, *Arts and Preaching*, 144.

defy immediate meaning, and to create distance from traditional categories of reflection.[29]

WRITING A FASHIONISTA SERMON

I now urge us to take a bold step toward an endeavor that may seem unfriendly. In reading the Bible, seeking a multifaceted communication with God necessitates turning away from the God we think we know—the God we have experienced or heard of—and instead opening ourselves to the possibility of encountering a God who can be revealed beyond the limits of reason and imagination.[30]

1) *Choosing a Text*

The pericope of the so-called "adulterous woman" (John 7:53—8:11) is included in Year C of the Revised Common Lectionary, specifically as a reading for the week of the Second Sunday of Lent. In approaching this text from a fashionista perspective, I sought to explore a theological movement from shedding shame to being clothed with life. Numerous debates surrounding the history of the reception of this pericope demonstrate that interpretations of the Bible have varied according to the understandings and values of the cultures engaging with the text—illustrating how the rejection or acceptance of a text "maps the borders of our subjectivities in the context of our cultural conditions of consumption (readership)."[31] For instance, Jesus' mercy toward a woman accused of adultery may have caused embarrassment within the early Christian community, possibly leading to concerns about weakening their strict penitential practices.[32] However, within the moral absolutes associated with patriarchal cultures, the significant danger faced by the woman when doubt was cast upon her adultery may have been given little consideration, even if she survived the ordeal.[33] Furthermore, while this pericope has traditionally been interpreted as a text focusing on ethical evaluation and salvation for the sinner, the impure intentions of the

---

29. Louw, "Preaching as Art."
30. Mitchell, *Meeting Mystery*, 68.
31. Guardiola-Sáenz, "Border-Crossing," 139. For example, Augustine was concerned that Jesus' forgiveness in this pericope might be interpreted as a tacit endorsement of adultery, which influenced the canonization process. Augustine, *Treatises on Marriage*, 107–8.
32. Gench, *Back to the Well*, 137.
33. Schottroff, *Lydia's Impatient Sisters*, 182.

accusers and the so-called righteous stoning carried out in the name of God have received minimal attention. The reception of this pericope would have had a specific ethical impact on its readers and communities, serving as a public demonstration of God's love, as presented in the Gospel of John, by following Jesus' example, regardless of the cost.[34]

2) *Reading with an Awareness of Where I Stand*

A preacher's experience and identity significantly influence how she reads the Bible, making it essential to recognize her own perspective. As I engaged with this text, I became another her and found myself standing on that runway, held up against my will, under a powerful gaze of shame and condemnation that transcends a myriad of emotions and facts.

3) *Reading with an Awareness of the Runway Where the Pericope and We Stand*

Although the story we read is part of John's Gospel, we need to recognize that the stigmatization of women (or the powerless) in the public sphere persists today within the context of deep-rooted social prejudices. Particularly in cases of sexual violence, the ubiquity of the internet and media has contributed to a secondary form of violence—the violence of exposure—which often intensifies the survivors' suffering.[35] There is also a risk that individuals may internalize the role of agents of justice, without recognizing its implicit intentions and biases. This naturally encompasses the complex

---

34. O'Day, "Gospel of John," 518–19. According to recent research in New Testament studies, various questions have been raised regarding the existence of the Johannine community or the audience of the Fourth Gospel. However, even if there was no specific receiving community, it is conceivable that there was a community that played a similar role in the process of the Gospel of John's acceptance into the canon. For instance, Jonathan Bernier's research suggests the possibility that the conflicts depicted in the aposynagōgos passages may not have arisen exclusively between the Jewish community and a specific Johannine community but rather could be attributed to conflicts experienced by followers of Jesus' message or their sympathizers ("A Mnemonic Community"). Bernier, *Aposynagōgos*, 132–34. Therefore, instead of referring to the existence of a sectarian Johannine community, it may be more possible to interpret these passages as alluding to conflicts that would have been experienced by recipients of John's Gospel who belonged to one of the broader Christian communities. In other words, when I use the term "community," I do not mean "one closed or narrow group" in a local sense, but rather, as Edward W. Klink III argues, a communal identity focused on reading and participating in the Gospel of John. Klink, *Sheep of the Fold*, 113–15.

35. "Cyber Violence Against Women."

and diverse interconnections of gender, cultural, economic, and political oppression. Preachers might reflect on how prejudice, exclusion, and violence manifest in their own communities.

4) *Reading with Fashio-Hermeneutic Perspective*

I engaged with the text not only through biblical Scriptures but also by incorporating insights from various artists, considering the illustrative, integrative, and intra-dynamic elements presented by Yang.[36] The painters' creative and imaginative responses to fashion were entirely different from the frightened and disheveled woman I initially envisioned.

Figure 1[37]

---

36. This analysis is based on my research, "When Lament Meets Shame-Ridden Suffering," presented at the 2023 annual meeting of Academy of Homiletics in Atlanta.

37. Giovanni Antonio Galli, *Cristo e l'adultera*, 1640, oil on canvas, 121 x 142 cm., Museo del Castelvecchio. Photograph by Sailko, Dec. 7, 2018. Licensed under Creative Commons Attribution-Share Alike 4.0 International (https://commons.wikimedia.org/wiki/File:Giovanni_antonio_galli,_cristo_e_l%27adultera,_dalla_coll._bernasconi_a_vr.jpg).

Figure 2[38]

a) Illustrative Reading

In Giovanni Antonio Galli's seventeenth-century painting *Cristo e l'adultera* (*Christ and the Woman Taken in Adultery*), the woman's attire is striking. Her hair is lustrous, appearing meticulously combed and groomed. Her garments are a light blue, silk-like fabric, not disheveled but instead complemented by luxuriously lustrous red robes. In the Middle Ages, blue dye was expensive, a color reserved for nobility and used as a celestial symbol to signify divine presence and intervention, as seen in the robes worn by emperors, saints, and the Virgin Mary.[39] Blue was a color imbued with moral connotations—this change in European society was largely due to the proliferation of moral discourse that dominated late medieval society and, above all, the views of the Protestant reformers of the sixteenth century regarding the social, religious, and artistic use of color.[40]

Pieter Brueghel the Younger's painting *Christ and the Woman Taken in Adultery* portrays a woman wearing in a luxurious blue robe, with neatly coiffed hair, layered pale pink garments, and shoes. She is also depicted

---

38. Pieter Brueghel the Younger, *Christ and the Woman Taken in Adultery*, 1600, oil on panel, 28.1 x 40.6 cm., Philadelphia Museum of Art (https://commons.wikimedia.org/wiki/File:Brueghel_II,_Pieter_-_Christ_and_the_Woman_Taken_in_Adultery_1600.jpg, public domain).

39. Pastoureau, *Blue*, 41.

40. Pastoureau, *Blue*, 40.

wearing a yellow walking gown that appears to be patterned. However, during this period, clothing featuring vibrant colors, stripes, plaids, and strong color contrasts was prohibited and deemed inappropriate for devout Christians. In other words, anything deemed too flashy or ostentatious was forbidden for those expected to embody dignity and modesty. This restriction applied not only to the clergy but also to widows, judges, and all government officials. As a result of these regulations, "the crippled, the deformed, lepers, the 'weak-bodied,' and those who were 'cretins and funny in the head' were compelled to wear their own often bright colors" throughout Europe.[41] This suggests that the desire to distinguish non-Christians, particularly in light of the prohibition on intermarriage between Christians and non-Christians reinstated by the Fourth Lateran Council in 1215, was a driving force behind these mandatory color laws.[42] This situation is not surprising when considering Tertullian's association of fashion with Eve's participation in original sin, and Barth's connection of it with the "demonic kingdom."[43] Color was, therefore, a crucial aspect of the "distinction" imposed upon marginalized and excluded groups in medieval society. In this context, fashion served not as a means of self-expression but as a tool of imposed identity—a form of stigmatization—expressed through discriminatory markings and shame.

In this context, artworks depicting fashion invite us to reflect on the shame, discrimination, distinction, exclusion, and marginalization experienced by the woman caught between execution and life. These representations prompt us to consider whether the luxurious colors and the portrayal of clothing deemed irreverent function as a deliberate form of "resistance," alongside the silencing of women.[44] Artists have often portrayed this woman with compassion, but in the case of these two painters, they appear to have adopted a more radical approach, incorporating their own responses to the subtle narrative that objectifies women and erases their agency.[45] This sense of resistance redirects our focus to the posture of Jesus, who refused to conform to the accusations and gaze of those surrounding the woman.

---

41. Pastoureau, *Blue*, 91.

42. Refer to Grayzel, *Church and the Jews*, 59–70. Grayzel also notes that "the Kalif's regulation required that unbelievers wear a different type of head-gear and girdle, and a patch on the upper garment or on the shoulders, which in the case of the Jews was to be yellow, in the case of the Christians blue, and in the case of the Magi black" (p. 61).

43. Tertullian, "On the Apparel of Women," 14; Barth, *Christian Life*, 229, 235.

44. One might suspect that the painters intended to depict her as lacking dignity and modesty. However, considering that her clothing does not sharply contrast with those of the surrounding figures, including Jesus, the scribes, and the Pharisees, it is reasonable to speculate that the opposite was intended.

45. O'Day, "Gospel of John," 523; Kim, *Woman and Nation*, 117.

b) Integrative Reading

Jesus' physical act of "bending" plays a significant role in this reading, as it embodies a crucial theological point. If the incarnation is central to the narrative of Jesus in the Gospel of John, then salvation, according to John, is found not apart from the body but in and through the body.[46] Furthermore, it is not only Jesus' posture that warrants attention but also the posture of the woman. The Bible uses the term "στήσαντες" (have set or placed) to describe her stance.[47] The contrast between the woman's standing posture and Jesus' bent posture carries theological implications.

Firstly, through his act of bending, Jesus divides, mixes, and transforms the space where his fashion is projected. When Jesus bends down and (lowers his head and) writes on the ground, he effectively redirects the accusation by shifting the accusers' attention from the woman to himself—thereby upholding the woman's dignity and fostering a sense of solidarity by absorbing the gaze that was directed toward her.[48] Moreover, Jesus' posture may be understood as a physical expression of distinguishing his position from that of the accusers, which prevents the escalation of their hostility by destabilizing the expected confrontational dynamics.[49]

Secondly, to rethink Jesus' silence, consider the Marc Jacobs fall 2017 runway show, held at the Park Avenue Armory. The show featured no music, set design, or additional embellishments; this deliberate choice emphasized the clothing and models, creating a stark and focused atmosphere.[50] Shairah Thoufeekh described this particular runway as stripped down to the bare essentials, devoid of the glamour or showmanship typically associated with Fashion Week. Alyssa Vingan Klein of *Fashionista* observed that the quietest expressions often made the most significant impact: a silent show rescues the clothes and the designer's intentions from the frenzy of flashmobs eager to capture every moment on their mobile devices.[51] The accusers challenge Jesus to disregard the voice, identity, and boundaries of the woman they have marginalized. They demand that Jesus clarify whose side he is on.[52] Jesus is invited to join the group of people who condemn the woman as her

---

46. O'Day, "Gospel of John," 519.

47. Many versions, including the New Revised Standard Version, translate it as "they made her stand."

48. Swartley, *John*, 212.

49. Joplin, "Intolerable Language," 232; Gench, "John 7:53," 398; Deans, "Rhetoric of Jesus," 414.

50. Thoufeekh, "Marc Jacobs." Also refer to "Runway Fall 2017."

51. Klein, "Marc Jacobs."

52. Guardiola-Sáenz, "Border-Crossing," 146.

judge. However, Jesus' silence serves as a rejection of this role as the enforcer of Jewish male authority—he refuses to offer comfort to those harmed by the woman's alleged adultery.[53] Through Jesus' silence, Jesus communicates something profound about the meaning and method of God's salvation in the midst of violence.[54] Jesus' response of silence, functioning as a "pause," effectively reverses the dynamic by halting the "clothing of violence and death upon her" propagated by the accusers.[55] Jesus creates a zone of silence between his communication and that of her accusers.[56] This silence between discourses represents a gap through which oppressive regimes can be challenged and overthrown—a space that allows for reflection, transformation, and the breaking of the patriarchal ideology underlying such actions.[57] Kathleen O'Connor argues that "God's silence gives reverence to voices of anger and resistance, of hope and despair."[58]

Lastly, the silence of the woman in John 8 can also be interpreted from various perspectives. Her silence appears to result from external factors, imposed by social or religious norms; she is constrained to define herself by the charges others have imposed upon her.[59] This woman could have been treated as a possession of a man, potentially subjected to sexual assault or forced into unhealthy sexual relations.[60] One might even argue that her silence serves as a form of resistance to the injustice imposed upon her.[61] Through Jesus' silence and bending, however, the sentence of shame and death imposed upon the woman is taken off, and she is clothed with the life bestowed by Jesus himself. Power is reversed, and theology is unsettled. The woman might have confessed, "While I feel cloaked with shame, God is tenderly stitching me a suit of clothes. The clothing is God's own self."[62]

c) Intra-Dynamic Reading (Including Communicating with Today)

Preachers do not simply read the text as a historical narrative; rather, they can engage with the biblical text as an active participant in the dialogue and

---

53. Schottroff, *Lydia's Impatient Sisters*, 185.
54. O'Sullivan, "Reading John 7:53," 3.
55. Guardiola-Sáenz, "Border-Crossing," 148.
56. Guardiola-Sáenz, "Border-Crossing," 147.
57. Guardiola-Sáenz, "Border-Crossing," 148.
58. O'Connor, "Voices Arguing," 29.
59. Kinukawa, "On John 7:53," 91.
60. Choi, *Women in the New Testament*, 98–101.
61. Han, *When Women Read*, 166.
62. Winner, *Wearing God*, 60.

action surrounding violence against women. This engagement encourages reflection on how the violence inflicted upon a woman labeled as an adulteress—shamed and threatened—might be transformed.[63]

At that time, the Pharisees held not only prominent positions within local synagogues but also high offices within the Jewish temple-state.[64] It is plausible that they orchestrated a confrontation with Jesus regarding the correct interpretation of Jewish law as a means to challenge his leadership. The charge of adultery was likely used as a pretext to test Jesus and potentially provide grounds for legal charges against him (John 8:6).[65] The presence of two credible witnesses to substantiate the charge of adultery suggests the possibility of a contrived scenario, possibly with the consent of the husband.[66] Moreover, the temple could serve as a poignant reminder to women of their social limitations and vulnerability.[67] Temple protocols contribute to the shame and humiliation experienced by women by imposing a series of restrictions that prevent them from accessing certain areas, including regulations related to menstruation and childbirth.[68] O'Day portrays this woman as "an object on display, given no name, no voice, no identity apart from that for which she stands accused."[69] However, Jesus' question provides the woman with the space to respond and choose life, enabling her to imagine stripping away the oppression and death imposed upon her and clothing life instead. The woman, whose identity as an "adulteress" has been clothed by the accusations of others, is now empowered by Jesus' clothedness to establish her own boundaries, negotiate her own existence, to express what Jesus has bestowed upon her, to participate in his clothedness, and walk into life independently.[70] By restoring value and dignity to the woman's life, she becomes a witness to Jesus' identity and justice.[71]

Furthermore, modern readers are invited to consider how this woman's story can redescript our world today.[72] The vocation of the text is to remain faithful to the world of "desire and possibility" that Jesus projects within it, understanding the text as a dynamic medium that requires constant

---

63. Schneiders, *Revelatory Text*, 182.
64. Horsley, "Synagogues in Galilee," 64.
65. Beasley-Murray, *John*, 146.
66. For more detail, refer to Weren, "Use of Violence," 133–34.
67. O'Sullivan, "Reading John 7:53," 2.
68. Manus and Ukaga, "Narrative of the Woman," 66.
69. O'Day, "John 7:53—8:11," 632.
70. Mudimeli and van der Westhuizen, "Unheard Voices," 120.
71. Young, "Two Anonymous Women," 60.
72. Schneiders, *Revelatory Text*, 182.

reaffirmation.[73] Susan Brooks Thistlethwaite notes that this story is the biblical text with which women who have suffered physical violence most often identify: "Women who have suffered physical violence hear that, while human law or custom may legitimize violence against women, such violence cannot stand in the face of God's affirmation of all humanity."[74]

Mirroring is present in Jesus' rhetoric: seeing women in the Bible who are silenced by shame and violence offers a valuable lens for examining ourselves and our communities. Merleau-Ponty suggests that awareness of one's limitations arises when one perceives the gaze of the other upon oneself.[75] Recognizing and evaluating the secondary knowledge gained about oneself through the eyes of others seems to be a matter of personal choice. However, this self-aware subjectivity may be ineffective in preventing actual violence when one is situated within power dynamics and is constantly and overwhelmingly threatened by violence. Even if one possesses agency, the capacity to act may be hindered. Moreover, individuals in oppressive situations often require both internal motivation and external validation to make sense of their existence. The accusers ceased throwing stones and turned away because Jesus' perceptions and actions compelled them to confront their own limitations. It underscores the notion that everyone is capable of any experience because everyone is, in some way, broken.[76] To be called to love "one another" (John 13:34; 15:12) is to acknowledge that just as loving someone is akin to loving oneself, so too is condemning another akin to condemning oneself, recognizing that one cannot be free from one's own sinfulness. It involves discovering a relational capacity for one another by recognizing the divinity inherent in all beings.[77]

---

73. O'Sullivan, "Reading John 7:53," 5.
74. Thistlethwaite, "Every Two Minutes," 102.
75. Merleau-Ponty, *Phenomenology of Perception*, 458.
76. Bondi, *To Pray*, 112.
77. Harvie, "Political Lament," 428.

SERMON PLANNING WORKSHEET

1. TEXT	John 7:53—8:11 (primarily employs *Dual Symbolism*)	
2. PRELIMINARY EXEGESIS	1) *Unit*	The pericope of the woman caught in adultery
	2) *Context*	The scribes and Pharisees accuse a woman of adultery to test Jesus with the law of Moses
	3) *Characters and Objects*	A woman accused of adultery, Jesus, the crowd, and participants of the sermon
	4) *Plot*	Jesus strips away the shame and clothes the woman with life
	5) *Timing*	During the Second Week of Lent (Year C)
	6) *Message*	God strips away our shame and clothes us with life (Godself)
3. ENCOUNTERING THE WORD	Bending down, Silence *Note: This sermon focuses on Jesus' action and posture*	
4. FASHION	1) Alexander McQueen's Autumn/Winter 1995 collection 2) Two paintings depicting "The Adulterous Woman" by Giovanni Antonio Galli and Pieter Brueghel 3) Käthe Kollwitz's *Pietà*	
5. FASHIONISTA HERMENEUTICS	Based on illustrative, integrative, and intra-dynamic reading (see above)	
6. SERMON FORM	Weaving a story of fashion, a biblical story, an illustrative metaphor, an integrative intervention, a theological metaphor, an intra-dynamic sense	

SAMPLE SERMON

"Jesus' Way of Clothing Us"

[Weaving a story of fashion] The realm of fashion and its expressions is so diverse that it can sometimes be challenging to communicate effectively through it. Such was the case with Alexander McQueen's Autumn/Winter 1995 collection, "Highland Rape." McQueen presented models on the runway depicting a bruised, beaten, and torn state to protest the British exploitation of Scotland in the eighteenth and nineteenth centuries and the romanticization of Scottish clothing by designers for financial gain.[78] However, his attempt was interpreted by audiences as "depicting a woman who had been raped," sparking controversy for its perceived objectification of women.[79]

[Weaving a biblical story] Whatever McQueen's intentions were, today's reading from John's Gospel also invites us onto a similarly chaotic runway. John 7:53—8:11 has long been used to convict women of adultery; perhaps the designer who brought this text to the runway sought to resist the social practice of accusing women through the misuse of patriarchal laws. Patriarchal marriage laws, deeply connected to men's honor and women's chastity, made even the slightest suspicion a deadly threat. A woman caught in this peril would struggle to shake the shame and fear from her memory for the rest of her life, even if she survived. The accusers and the community, in the name of God, clothed themselves in their own "righteousness" and willingly chose the "judging stone." The woman was reduced to an object, a spectacle, and a decoy to entrap Jesus—a passive participant in a life-and-death controversy imposed by her accusers, both psychologically and physically.

[Weaving an illustrative metaphor] (see figures 1 and 2) Giovanni Antonio Galli's and Pieter Brueghel's depictions of the woman present a contrast to McQueen's attempt. The woman is portrayed with lustrous hair that appears meticulously combed and groomed. Her unruffled, light blue, silk-like garments are beautifully complemented by a luxuriously lustrous red robe. The blue dye, often used to depict medieval emperors or the saintly Virgin Mary, lends the woman an almost saintly appearance. However, considering that clothing featuring vibrant colors, stripes, checks, and strong contrasts was forbidden at the time and deemed inappropriate—especially for devout Christians—and recognizing that the use of color was a crucial aspect of ethics for distinguishing marginalized and excluded groups in medieval society, this attire can also be interpreted as a form of resistance against an imposed identity, a "stigma" expressed through discriminatory markings and shame. How can the woman, standing at the threshold of

---

78. Hurtado, "Autumn/Winter 1995." For a detailed image, see Bolton, *Alexander McQueen*, 125.

79. Hurtado, "Autumn/Winter 1995."

death, stand firm against the painful clothing of shame, discrimination, distinction, exclusion, and marginalization?

[**Weaving an integrative intervention**] What must it have been like for Jesus to witness the roar and wickedness of accusations, with a woman clothed in shame from head to toe, awaiting death? In an effort to protect his image (the woman) from the glaring flashes of judgment, Jesus silences. In the stillness, Jesus bends at the waist. This act of bending was akin to "wearing mourning," like donning a black dress and black bracelets, or, in the Korean tradition, a hairpin with a white ribbon.[80] Could it be that Jesus intended to convey his grief over the woman's suffering, as Jesus felt her shame was like a crown of thorns encircling her entire body? Mourning attire typically signals that one is in lamenting, and this silent expression demands that others recognize and appropriately respect the grief. Jesus prepares his mourning clothes by bowing low and choosing silence in the presence of a woman already facing a death sentence. Whether or not the people recognized Jesus' actions as mourning, that silence and bending carried the power to halt the accusations, focus attention, and pause further harassment.

[**Weaving a theological metaphor**] *Pietà* is the Italian word for sorrow and lamentation, normally referring to works depicting the Virgin Mary holding the dead body of Jesus. Among the many Pietà works, a notable piece by the German artist Käthe Kollwitz (1867–1945) carries a deeply personal story: Kollwitz's youngest son, Peter, was killed in World War I, and her grandson Peter, named after her son, was killed in World War II.[81] Kollwitz's *Pietà* is placed in a room with a perforated ceiling, leaving it defenselessly exposed to the elements—not only sunlight but also wind, snow, and rain. A mother who cradles her son's entire body with her own endures alongside him the snow when it falls, the rain when it pours, and the wind when it blows.

Kollwitz's *Pietà* seems to embody the many lives lost, defenselessly exposed to the winds of history, and a God who participates in their suffering and clothes those who endure adversity with Godself. It evokes the image of Jesus, who bore the weight of all accusations alongside the woman, who remained silent in lamentation, and who bent low to redirect the gaze of those who judged the woman clothed in shame and suffering toward himself.

---

80. Winner, *Wearing God*, 42.
81. Kang, "Comforting All the Parents."

Figure 4[82]

[**Weaving an intra-dynamic sense**] Jesus' runway does not culminate in resistance or silence; rather, he strips the woman of the tangled garments of power, condemnation, and death, and clothes her anew, knowing that God's law always sustains life at every level.[83] It was only after all those who had surrounded and condemned her (in the midst of being, ἐν μέσῳ οὖσα) had dispersed that Jesus finally stood upright (John 8:9b–10a). Jesus quietly asks her a question, breaking the breathless silence, and she responds, "No one" (John 8:11a). Jesus asks nothing more of her—he doesn't inquire about her feelings regarding the accusation, nor does he leave her to relive the traumatic experience alone.[84] Instead, Jesus bears the suffering and death inflicted upon her to declare, "Neither do I condemn you" (John 8:11a). In this moment, she transitions from condemnation to acquittal and life. Jesus refuses to choose between the two, allowing an encounter with the mind and intentions of God on a phenomenal level—beyond the human

---

82. Käthe Kollwitz, *Pietà* (1920). Image courtesy of Wikimedia Commons. Licensed under Creative Commons Attribution-Share Alike 3.0 Unported License (https://commons.wikimedia.org/wiki/File:K%C3%A4the_Kollwitz,_Pieta.JPG).

83. Rabie-Boshof, "Pericope Adulterae," 17.

84. Toensing, "Divine Intervention," 167.

dimension and our attempts to comprehend it through human thought and emotion—while simultaneously halting the prescribed execution of women and caring for her shame and trauma. Jesus stripped himself of his glory and took on human form, devising a way to reclothe us in the glory that was stripped away by our shame and failures.[85] We do not know the details of the life the woman gained afterward, but we do know that, like her, in the midst of unbearable days of shame and pain, we are called to shed the garments clothed upon us and put on the garments of "life" that Jesus has given us. It is also clear that, in the midst of our recurring moments of suffering, Jesus bestows upon us the Holy Spirit to renew our garments continuously, day by day, forever. This garment, clothed by Christ, is not intended for "distinction." Christ's actions caused the woman and the crowd gathered there to think in a new way and to give life to one another in a new manner. It is "Jesus' way of wearing us" that dissolves the distinctions between sinner and saint, sacred and profane, righteous and unrighteous (cf. Gal 3:28); rather, it fosters a connection. Jesus' act of clothing us liberates us, transforms our perception of our bodies and souls, and alters the way we communicate with ourselves and others. Jesus' clothing us is also an invitation to participate in Christ's deep heart and act to clothe others. We are called to clothe those in need (Matt 25:35–36). We are invited to participate in God's hospitality, healing, and life-giving work. We are called to live fully within the overflowing fullness of the God who clothes us.

This is because Jesus clothes us—abundantly and eternally.

CONCLUSION

I want to return to the question raised in the introduction: humans have long communicated through the language of dress. These messages can be communicated effectively or poorly, much like verbal communication.

Can we truly see and respond to someone's sartorial statements as sincerely as Jesus did? While we aspire to do so, we must acknowledge that we are not Jesus. How should we respond, and what gestures can we make, when we encounter someone whose clothing is particularly torn and tattered, signaling an urgent need for something new?

One could argue that the spirituality of aesthetics contributes to the broadening of our horizons, opening up new perspectives on the sacred dimensions of life.[86] It even fosters a new relationship with space and the divine, penetrating the realm of the incomprehensible and revealing

---

85. Winner, *Wearing God*, 35.
86. Louw, "Preaching as Art."

indicators that can guide humans in their search for meaning, resilience, strength, and trust.

In many cases, it is not necessary and impossible for the preacher to interpret and conclude all the biblical possibilities. By leaving the aesthetic sensibility open, participants in the sermon are invited to respond creatively and imaginatively in their own way. This approach can lead to a meaningful engagement with the sermon, even if it does not result in universal understanding or unanimity. This is because the essence of this approach to preaching lies in fostering unexpected communication, rather than imposing a one-sided authoritative interpretation.

4

Film & Preaching

Chris Murphy

INTRODUCTION

In many ways, watching a film is society's most common way to see and listen to a type of sermon. Movie producer George Miller says that "cinema storytellers have become the new priests."[1] Screenplays are the new sermons and movies and sermons have a similar purpose of helping people connect to the divine, whether they are aware of God or not. As Sunggu Yang suggests about movies in his book *Arts and Preaching: An Aesthetic Homiletic for the Twenty-First Century*, we live in a society that enjoys the arts and finds in them an experience of the transcendent.[2]

Film may be the most common art form that people enjoy. It is common for people to watch multiple films each week from home as well as to occasionally enjoy movies in a movie theater, which serves as an alternative location from church to hold communal experiences where the transcendent becomes known. It is culturally obvious that far more people are attracted to movies than to church worship services. In *Reel Spirituality*, Robert K. Johnston reminds us of the fascination that famous director Martin Scorsese felt when he first entered a movie theater. "The first sensation was that of entering a magical world—the soft carpet, the smell of fresh

---

1. Johnston, *Reel Spirituality*, 28.
2. Yang, *Arts and Preaching*, 96.

popcorn, the darkness, the sense of safety, and, above all, sanctuary—much the same in my mind, as entering a church. A place of dreams. A place that excited and stretched my imagination."[3] Scorsese, a devout Catholic, grew up with an appreciation both for church and movies, but for many today hearing a sermon is far less attractive than exploring the latest movies in the theater or on Netflix, Amazon Prime, HBO (Max), or a host of other sites. Hear what Yang has to say:

> If a movie's world is spiritual, aesthetic, and revelatory enough to invoke people's transcendent experience, and that movie's revelatory event becomes involved in the communication and communion with the audience's everyday life, we can convincingly contend that what the (sacred) work film does for its audience is identical to what preaching does for its congregation.[4]

If the goal of a film and a sermon are identical, one might wonder which does a better job at helping people experience God's transcendent presence. A case could be made that the creativity in films exceeds the creativity in many sermons. Some might even say that watching a movie helps them experience God more than hearing a sermon. A good preacher might wish to explore whether the development of a sermon could be enhanced by learning how films are formed. In this chapter, we will be exploring a new paradigm for preaching based on the method of sharing a story that we see in films. Drawing from the work of Yang, we will call this style a cinemate homiletic.

It may be helpful to know that I am reflecting on the connection of film and preaching from the perspective of a pastor of a small church in Newberg, Oregon, near George Fox University. I recognize that the college students who live a few blocks from my church are more interested in the latest movie than my preaching. These students are exploring spiritual meaning in many ways. One way to engage the spiritual journeys of young adults and others in my community is to explore with them the integration of film with Scripture through the art form of preaching within the context of a worshiping community called to mission both locally and globally.

Exploring film through preaching is not so much a technique to get people to come to church. Rather it is an opportunity to follow the movement of the Holy Spirit who is engaging people regularly through film. Connecting film and preaching is being faithful to the movement of God's revelation in our world. I also am aware that like film, preaching is an art form that requires creativity. For me, exploring film and preaching is a way

---

3. Johnston, *Reel Spirituality*, 28.
4. Yang, *Arts and Preaching*, 98.

for me to expand my own creative skills and to be open to how the Holy Spirit may wish to stretch my growth as a preacher. As a pastor, I am not trying to compete with popular culture and film, but I am trying to stay current to how people are shaped spiritually, and I wish to be open to how the Holy Spirit is using film to awaken people to the transcendent.

Figure 1[5]

THE ART FORM OF PREACHING AND FILM

There are many considerations for the preacher in choosing how to incorporate the art form of preaching with the art form of film. We will discuss three current methods and how one might integrate all three into a potential sermon. We begin with discussing how to choose the appropriate film to use in a sermon.

---

5. "Captivated Movie Audience," public domain image (https://stockcake.com/i/captivated-movie-audience_355838_498051).

Choosing a Film

Preachers are encouraged to choose films for use in preaching that are well known by their congregation and popular in the broader culture. In Yang's book *Arts and Preaching* he highlights that pop movies are the best choice because they are the movies that most churchgoers are likely to watch.

The goal is to choose good movies. According to Yang, good movies are "easy to watch, yet deep enough to require ardent reflection on life."[6] Preachers need to be careful in choosing films that connect to the congregation and that ultimately affirm the values of the gospel of Jesus Christ. Preachers need to engage movies with an eye to see the sacred wisdom within the stories rather than with initial feelings of judgment or religious critique.

One must approach film as a deeply sacred way that people are engaging in creative expression of the human experience. In choosing a helpful film for a sermon, it is important to be culturally sensitive and conscious of the qualities that make a film great. Films that will resonate with congregations often engage in questions of life's meaning and the value of love and faith. A good film will explore both the vulnerability of human experience and the triumph of the human spirit. Films that directly or indirectly explore spirituality as a theme or the plight of oppressed people often align well to being integrated into a sermon.

The Spirituality of Film and Preaching

Spirituality writers are fond of saying that everything is spiritual. A spiritual worldview engages all of life with an eye to perceive the movement of the Holy Spirit and the goodness of creation. From a spiritual perspective then we may also recognize that the divine is always engaging creation with love and guidance.

Within this context, it becomes apparent that watching a film provides the opportunity to engage in an awareness of the transcendent. Reflecting later about a film in conversation with another person or in conversation with God may be a meaningful way to hear God's wisdom and to enjoy God's presence through the gift of film. Talking about spirituality related to film or other art forms may seem like a stretch for people who connect spirituality to the institution of the Christian church or other religious institutions. The reality is that spirituality is a major theme in every art form, from film to music, to literature and beyond. We need to open to the reality that God is active in the world beyond Sunday morning church. Rather than popular

---

6. Yang, *Arts and Preaching*, 94.

culture being in opposition to Christian worship, it is far more engaging to look for ways that culture and the arts connect spirituality and enhance the spiritual growth of people. Certainly, some expressions of art are not life giving, but the church needs to swim in the stream of art to both connect to the transcendent in art and to help people discern the expressions of art that lead to life and wholeness.

Spirituality as a field is less defined by specific doctrine and belief than by human experience of the divine. For this reason, a spiritual perspective provides a broad canvas from which art may explore the sacred and divine within creation. Since the church has often been critiqued for creating confining beliefs, engagement with film helps the church to become more open to spiritual experiences that are part of the daily reality of churchgoers and others as well.

Introducing a Cinemate Homiletic

The three main approaches to incorporating the art form of film into the task of preaching include the movie illustration approach, the message-filming approach, and the dialogical approach. A cinemate homiletic approach may be understood as a type of integration of the best of these approaches. We will explore all three approaches and synthesize them into the cinemate homiletic method.

The Movie Illustration Approach

The classic way preachers use films as part of sermons is by film clips. Like other illustrations within sermons, the film clips may be useful to highlight a point that the preacher is making related to an insight from Scripture. For example, to highlight the power of love from 1 Corinthians 13, one might show a film clip that demonstrates love in action. The purpose of the film clip is limited to the key ideas of the sermon being drawn from a particular Scripture passage. The film clip normally is under five minutes long, so as not to detract from the larger portion of the sermon.

The value of the sermon illustration is that it shows the preacher's interest in engaging with the broader popular culture and the church's commitment to exploring God's communication through art forms like film. The creativity in the film clip will often inspire the congregation to connect to God and to gain a deeper appreciation for the message in the sermon and particularly in the Scripture passage for the morning.

The danger of movie clips could be if they dominate the sermon in a way that distracts from the Scripture or the ideas of the preacher. The other challenge may be finding an appropriate film clip for the idea being presented or accidentally poorly interpreting the theme or insight from a film.

Regardless of the risks in using film clips, the value of connecting the congregation with a positive experience with film is worth the effort a preacher makes to incorporate film clips occasionally into sermons. As thoughtful and engaging as a preacher might be in reflecting on a film, there is a powerful benefit in showing film clips because they allow a congregation to engage with that art form of film in a more direct way.

Again, film clips are not used simply to show a preacher is relevant with popular culture; this would be akin to a preacher wearing blue jeans in order to look young and hip. No, the reason to use film clips is because film is an amazing medium for people to experience the transcendent. Back in the day, there were movie review television shows with people like Siskel and Ebert who would show a film clip and then share a conversation about the value of a film. In the same way in a sermon a film clip can capture the attention of the congregation and provide the appropriate environment to explore the transcendent spiritual insights that can come from a film. Without the film clip, a congregation may use its imagination, but I think a clip helps make the sermon come alive in a fresh, creative way that allows people to feel God's presence through film.

A practical aspect of using a film clip is having proper copyright privileges, but films are used in many other academic contexts, so churches are also able to have access to film clips with proper planning.

The Message Filming Approach

Another meaningful way to engage the art of film with writing a sermon is to have the style of a sermon be similar to the screenplay of a film as well as the approach a director might make in creating a film. Using insights from film studies and theory, a preacher may write an engaging reflection on a story connected to Scripture and have it be preached in a way that is similar to the flow and creativity of a film. This way of preaching seeks to be visual and engage other senses as well. The benefit of this style is that it potentially might bring to life God's word in a similar way that film brings to life the stories that shape our lives. Although a film clip might accent this approach, film clips are not necessary for this style of preaching.

This approach to writing a sermon also lends itself to creating a manuscript that is written intentionally with a narrative style that engages an audience. This is similar to how a monologue functions in a play. The proper screenplay-styled sermon will create energy, suspense, and other emotional responses. The sermon using this style will feel dramatic and the preacher may seek to almost engage the manuscript as an actor explores a script. This approach could include first-person dialogue as if the preacher is a character in Scripture. It might also mirror a specific genre of film, such as comedy, drama, or action.

Depending on how it is designed the message filming approach might look similar to a specific film or it may sound like a film but be simply telling a Scripture story with a more creative style.

The Dialogical Approach

The third approach to preaching using film involves engaging in a dialogue between a film and a Scripture passage. This involves providing an overview of a particular movie, while also referencing key portions within the movie that have significance for the plot and the deeper revelatory purpose of the film. Then the preacher connects the story and insights of the film to the Scripture passage, which may also be a story. The choice of the film and its theme should align with the wisdom of the Scripture passage. For example, a story of Jesus feeding the five thousand might connect to a movie that includes acts of generosity that benefit people living in poverty. One example of a film with generosity as a theme is *Chocolat* (2000) starring Juliette Binoche and Johnny Depp. In the film a small group of compassionate townspeople reach out to the visitors that arrive at the shore of the river in houseboats, while others in the community treat these same strangers as dangerous threats to the town's safety. The use of chocolate recipes to bring people together engages the senses and brings creativity and joy to the film.

In his book *Hearing a Film, Seeing a Sermon*, Timothy Cargal effectively introduces this dialogical approach to preaching through the use of popular films. He includes examples of sermons where classic films like *Spider-Man* (2002) and *Bruce Almighty* (2003) are paired with Scripture stories to provide engaging reflection. Cargal uses films alongside liturgical readings and chooses films that particularly relate to scriptural themes.

Cargal suggests that film clips are not needed or recommended for this approach to preaching.[7] He is concerned that a sermon is too short a time to effectively introduce a film clip without detracting from the sermon itself. I understand his reservations, but I think a short clip may be effective

---

7. Cargal, *Hearing a Film*, 48.

in supporting a dialogical approach to preaching as long as it highlights the central idea of the sermon.

The beauty of dialogical preaching is that a good portion of the content of the film may be described in the sermon. Quotes of different characters may be shared and people will be inspired by hearing the sermon. One challenge to this approach is that in order to engage a film well, the plot of the film usually needs to be revealed, so the preacher runs the risk of spoiling the movie for those who have not seen the film and wish to watch it without hearing the plot or knowing the ending. For this reason, the dialogical film approach may be best used with films that are popular and that have been out long enough that the majority of people will have seen them.

The best films will be the ones that fit with your audience. For a younger audience, it may be best to use films within the last five to ten years rather than classic films from the past that might appeal more to an older congregation. Although many age groups enjoy films, each congregation will have its own culture and some films may be more effective depending on the interests of the church. Normally, preaching with the use of film appeals especially to congregations that wish to engage popular culture and who are seeking to grow younger and more connected to the interests of younger people or a society that enjoys entertainment through movies. Since many people experience film in a spiritual way, where God's presence is felt through dramatized stories, then it is wise to see film as a wonderful dialogue partner in a sermon. A sermon that engages a film well will provide an opportunity for the Holy Spirit to touch hearts and shape people spiritually in a profound way.

A NEW CINEMATE APPROACH TO PREACHING AND FILM

A new approach to integrating film and preaching is described by Yang in his book *Arts and Preaching*. Yang integrates the three other approaches to using film into a fourth style called the cinemate approach, also described as the cinemate narrative-hermeneutical methodology. One aspect of Yang's approach uses five cinemate-sociospiritual codes as an interpretive hermeneutic on Scripture. The sociospiritual codes provide a cinemate biblical hermeneutic. The sociospiritual codes are drawn from the field of film studies and often shape the discussion of film by writers. The five sociospiritual codes are: the Code of Gender and Sex; the Code of Power, Good, and Evil; the Code of Humanity and Divinity; the Code of Money and the Material; and the Code of Nature and Violence.[8]

8. Yang, *Arts and Preaching*, 34.

The Code of Gender and Sex

This code involves movies whose themes specifically explore gender or sex issues. We notice that these films explore many significant topics, like the role of women in society, the value of inclusion of the LGBTQ+ community, and the values of sexuality and intimacy as part of the human experience of meaningful relationships. Examples of movies that explore the code of gender and sex include *Thelma and Louise* (1991), *Philadelphia* (1993), *Milk* (2008), *The Graduate* (1967), *Sex and the City* (movie versions: 2008 and 2010), and *Don't Worry Darling* (2022). Like other topics presented in movies, one is struck by the truth that movies often explore the topic of gender and sex much more thoroughly and thoughtfully than in sermons. This might be a reflection on how diverse congregational views are on sex and gender and that the intergenerational nature of congregations makes sexuality a challenging subject to bring up within a sermon. That being said, connecting a movie within a sermon might be an effective method to explore the topic of gender and sex within a church community.

The topic of human sexuality for many in church contexts raises questions and even psychological trauma. Many people who attend worship services repress sexual thoughts or feelings for fear that church is not a safe place to explore the topic of human sexuality. When sexuality is brought up in sermons, the theme is often about how to address the sin of lust rather than the positive impact of sexuality and intimacy within healthy relationships. Preachers need creative ways to engage in a helpful conversation about human sexuality with a collaborative style that potentially incorporates both film and Scripture together.

The Code of Power, Good, and Evil

Many action films including superhero films like the Marvel series engage the topics of power, good, and evil. In the Marvel films, for example, the main characters demonstrate normal human characteristics but also superhuman power. There are usually both good characters and evil villains that engage in battles that determine the future of the world.

These film themes are excellent opportunities to engage in conversation with Scripture stories, where good and evil also coexist. One might imagine using the Old Testament story of David and Goliath to bridge with a film such as *Star Wars* (1977) to show the battle between good and evil. Sermons that incorporate the themes of power, good, and evil benefit from exploring the complexity of what makes a person good and why evil actions occur. Movies like *Lord of the Rings* (2001–3) helpfully depict even good characters like Frodo Baggins being tempted at times to succumb to evil. Stories where Jesus himself faces temptations parallel well movies where evil seeks to weaken good characters.

The Code of Humanity and Divinity

This code is used in films that wish to explore ways in which characters demonstrate God-like qualities and human strengths and limitations. One of the great gifts that film and literature provide people is the opportunity to watch fragile humanity navigate the struggles of life. Good films do not show people waltzing through life with ease, success, and actions of pure virtue. Engaging films rather show the failure of humanity to live up to its sacred nature and the struggle of humanity to overcome obstacles including those that are self-inflicted.

For example, the movie *Rocky* (1976) depicts a struggling guy who is trying to become his best self. He seems to fail at everything, but with determination and the love of a shy woman named Adrian he eventually can compete at a high level as a boxer. Both Adrian and Rocky help each other become courageous human beings, but they are brought together through adversity.

In films that use the code of humanity and divinity there is also a sense that some divine force is at work to accomplish something beautiful. In the movie *Star Wars*, the force is the divine presence that guides Luke Skywalker to destroy the Death Star. In a movie like *Erin Brockovich* (2000), Julia Roberts plays a woman who uses her legal abilities to help support people in poverty who have become sick due to environment injustice. When the character of Erin eventually wins her cases and achieves financial benefit to hurting families while challenging big business, we sense the transcendent power of the divine in partnership with the courage of the human spirit.

In a sermon that explores the human and the divine it is helpful to highlight a perspective of Celtic Christian spirituality and other forms of Creation spirituality that recognize what is deepest in humanity is actually sacred or divine. Humanity is created in the image of God, so when we do the right thing we are in alignment with the divine nature. Other theologies might choose to emphasize the sinful nature of humanity instead, but whatever the pastor's theological perspective grace is often a key emphasis in sermons that explore the divine human connection. In good movies, grace is shown reflecting the unconditional love and forgiveness of God and the active power of God's love to overcome failure and loss.

The Code of Money and the Material

Films that introduce the code of money and material often have plots that highlight how money and material wealth lead to the corruption of people. Characters portray people who experience wealth and struggle to maintain morality or compassionate behavior. The movie *The Wolf of Wall Street* (2013) starring Leonardo di Caprio and Margot Robbie is a classic example of a person who gets over his head making money only to come crashing down when his legal mistakes catch up with him.

The movie *Elvis* (2022) also depicts how money and material wealth, with the added stress of a Las Vegas lifestyle that includes an addiction to drugs and sex, lead one of the greatest voices of a generation to die in his early forties. Movies that address money and material at times seem to glamorize the pursuit of wealth and fame, but in the end most of these films show the damage done to people who pursue wealth over the value of relationships. Fewer films about money and wealth show the benefit of wealth on society. One exception is the movie *Schindler's List* (1993), which tells the true story of Oskar Schindler, played by Liam Neeson, who used his wealth to help free Jewish children, women, and men during the Holocaust.

The Code of Nature and Violence

These films include significant violence and sometimes cataclysmic natural events that cause characters to struggle for survival and to do actions of violence that are unlikely unless circumstances are dire. One film that explores an apocalyptic end to the world is *Don't Look Up* (2021). In this film, two astronomers must share with the world that a comet will soon arrive and destroy planet Earth. In the film, humanity struggles to try to maintain life while facing impending death and destruction. Violence becomes a natural struggle as people try to hold on to some form of control and protection. In the end, the virtue of relationship again is lifted up as the deeper meaning of life.

Movies that depict natural disasters and physical violence run the risk of creating significant feelings of fear and anxiety. It is common for movie watchers to be desensitized from violence, which raises questions about whether movies particularly with graphic violence are more harmful than helpful. At the same time, violence is a reality in our world and exploring violence alongside the value of peace may enable movies to awaken people to what is most meaningful in life, which is the great question of spirituality.

APPLICATION OF THE CINEMATE SOCIOSPIRITUAL HERMENEUTIC

Now that we have explored the use of sociospiritual codes in the cinemate sociospiritual hermeneutic, we may suggest how to incorporate this approach into writing a sermon. First, one must choose a movie and determine what sociospiritual codes are most represented in the movie. Next, a Scripture may be chosen that mirrors similar themes from the movie chosen. Then, the plot of the movie is explored alongside the reflection on a particular Scripture story. Ultimately, a strong message about the gospel of Jesus Christ is integrated into both the reflection of the movie and the passage of Scripture.

An example on how to interpret cinemate sociospiritual codes may be found in the movie *Black Panther* (2018). In the movie *Black Panther*, the most relevant sociospiritual codes are the code of power, good, and evil and the code of humanity and divinity. The Black Panther character T'Challa is characterized as a good person who struggles to learn of his father's evil actions. This creates T'Challa's own struggle for identity as he seeks to be a wise leader. The Black Panther eventually demonstrates wisdom and strength and uses his power to defeat evil and bring about good. Another code, the code of humanity and divinity, is also relevant for the *Black Panther* movie. We see that the character of the Black Panther, due to the power received in drinking a special liquid of a vibranium plant, is able to demonstrate divine powers. The Black Panther even has the ability to visit the ancestral plane or heaven to connect to loved ones who have passed on from death to eternal life. The Black Panther explores the deep connection between divine and human abilities and how humanity seeks to live in a spiritual way while on earth.

Drawing from the study of the film *Black Panther* we will now choose a Scripture story that has a similar theme. Since the Black Panther character demonstrates a Christ-like image, it is natural to connect this movie to a story of Jesus. The resurrection story of Jesus from John 20:1–22 provides a nice parallel story to the movie, which will inspire listeners to follow Christ's mission in the world. Before seeing a summary sermon, we can look at an outline on how best to prepare and write a sermon that connects Scripture to a particular film.

SERMON PLANNING WORKSHEET

1. **Choose Film:** The best films are inspiring and easy for connecting themes to Scripture stories.
2. **Choose Text:** For sermons that include film reflection it is recommended to use a narrative text of Scripture, such as a story of Jesus.
3. **Analysis of Text:** Recognize the historical and cultural elements of the Scripture story. Choose a story that inspires you and those who will listen to the sermon. Understand the key plot line of the story and how it relates to a film or film clip.
4. **Analyze Film:** Review film summaries and identify film codes that are used. Understand film plot and theme.
5. **Theme:** What is the key idea of the Scripture story that you wish to highlight in relation to a film?
6. **Theology and Spirituality:** Choose a theological and/or spiritual insight that you wish to engage through the story and film.
7. **Mission:** What similar missional goals are shown in the Scripture story and film choice?
8. **Choose Film Clip:** Choose clip that specifically highlights the key theme or subtext of a film and that connects to your chosen Scripture story.

EXAMPLE OF SERMON PREPARATION

1. **Film choice is *Black Panther*:** Similar to story of Jesus and his resurrection, T'Challa, the main character of *Black Panther*, is a Christ-like figure who experiences a form of resurrection and goes on to lead his nation and bring compassion to the world.
2. **Scripture Text: John 20:1–22**—This passage is chosen because it highlights the power of the resurrection and mirrors the Christlike figure of the Black Panther.
3. **Analysis of Text:** This resurrection story of Jesus demonstrates Jesus' love and power and his desire to fulfill his mission of compassion and wholeness for the world.
4. **Analyze Film:** Analyze the film *Black Panther* and look at movie reviews. Determine the film codes related to *Black Panther*.

5. **Theme:** We wish to explore how *Black Panther* is a Christ-like story of resurrection.

6. **Theological and Spiritual Insight:** I wish to show that both the *Black Panther* movie and the John 20:1–22 story reveal the power of the resurrection and the power of love over hate and good over evil.

7. **Mission:** The mission of Christ to bring compassion and social justice to the world is shown in the resurrection story and the *Black Panther* movie.

8. **Movie Clip:** The movie clip chosen is the part where T'Challa goes to the ancestral plain and sees his dad near the end of the movie. He confronts his dad and then returns to serve as a Black Panther who will use the resources of Wakanda to serve the world.

SAMPLE SERMON

Scripture Text: John 20:1–22

The Resurrection of Jesus

Early on the first day of the week, while it was still dark, Mary Magdalene came to the tomb and saw that the stone had been removed from the tomb. So she ran and went to Simon Peter and the other disciple, the one whom Jesus loved, and said to them, "They have taken the Lord out of the tomb, and we do not know where they have laid him." Then Peter and the other disciple set out and went toward the tomb. The two were running together, but the other disciple outran Peter and reached the tomb first. He bent down to look in and saw the linen wrappings lying there, but he did not go in. Then Simon Peter came, following him, and went into the tomb. He saw the linen wrappings lying there, and the cloth that had been on Jesus' head, not lying with the linen wrappings but rolled up in a place by itself. Then the other disciple, who reached the tomb first, also went in, and he saw and believed, for as yet they did not understand the scripture, that he must rise from the dead. Then the disciples returned to their homes.

Jesus Appears to Mary Magdalene

But Mary stood weeping outside the tomb. As she wept, she bent over to look into the tomb, and she saw two angels in white sitting where the body of Jesus had been lying, one at the head and the other at the feet. They said to her, "Woman, why are you weeping?" She said to them, "They have taken away my Lord, and I do not know where they have laid him." When she had said this, she turned around and saw Jesus standing there, but she did not know that it was Jesus. Jesus said to her, "Woman, why are you weeping? Whom are you looking for?" Supposing him to be the gardener, she said to him, "Sir, if you have carried him away, tell me where you have laid him, and I will take him away." Jesus said to her, "Mary!" She turned and said to him in Hebrew, "Rabbouni!" (which means Teacher). Jesus said to her, "Do not touch me, because I have not yet ascended to the Father. But go to my brothers and say to them, 'I am ascending to my Father and your Father, to my God and your God.'" Mary Magdalene went and announced to the disciples, "I have seen the Lord," and she told them that he had said these things to her.

Jesus Appears to the Disciples
When it was evening on that day, the first day of the week, and the doors were locked where the disciples were, for fear of the Jews, Jesus came and stood among them and said, "Peace be with you." After he said this, he showed them his hands and his side. Then the disciples rejoiced when they saw the Lord. Jesus said to them again, "Peace be with you. As the Father has sent me, so I send you." When he had said this, he breathed on them and said to them, "Receive the Holy Spirit."

Sermon Title: Jesus and Black Panther

Sermon Introduction

One of the most influential films in recent years is the *Black Panther* movie, which came out in 2018 and had a sequel in 2022. The initial *Black Panther* movie is the story of T'Challa, who becomes the Black Panther after his father dies. The Black Panther is the leader of the Wakanda people, who are a highly technologically advanced people group in Africa. T'Challa is challenged for the throne in a ritual fight but wins over a chief from a mountain tribe. The Wakandan people live hidden from other nations and benefit from the natural resource of vibranium, which is only available in their region. The plot of the film is related to whether vibranium should become a resource that other nations should have available to them or whether

Wakanda needs to keep it a secret, so they can stay safe from the vulnerabilities of other nations.

Eventually Eric Stevens, also known as Killmonger, enters Wakanda looking for vibranium and his right to take the throne of Wakanda. The father of Stevens is T'Challa's deceased uncle and therefore Stevens is also in line to be considered for the throne. We learn later that T'Challa's father killed his own brother, T'Challa's uncle, in Oakland, which led to Eric Stevens growing up with anger over his father's death. In another ritual fight, Eric Stevens seemingly defeats T'Challa by throwing him over a cliff. Stevens is then allowed to become temporarily the next Black Panther and plans to use his power to provide weapons of destruction to aid other nations. This plan is dangerous because it threatens to start a huge global war.

The surprise of the film is that T'Challa, though presumed to be dead after falling from a cliff, is found alive but in a frozen coma. The mountain people find him and take him to the cliffs and caves where they live. T'Challa's loved ones visit the mountain tribe and are taken to T'Challa. He receives healing through a vibranium-infused heart shaped herb and is once again given power to lead his people as the Black Panther.

Eric Stevens with his Black Panther power takes on the newly healed Black Panther T'Challa in an epic battle. T'Challa eventually is victorious and the danger of a global war is averted. Rather than continuing to keep Wakanda hidden from other nations, the restored Black Panther shares the resource of vibranium with the world and uses its powerful technology to bring economic development to other nations, including the urban area of Oakland, California.

The part of the film that touches me the most is when T'Challa is given the herb that restores his strength. As part of the healing experience, he is transported to a spiritual world like heaven and sees his father, who has already died. His father is ready to welcome him into the ancestral plane of eternal life, but T'Challa confronts his father for his failure to provide vibranium to the world. With love for his father but also love for Wakanda and the world, T'Challa leaves the heavenly plain and wakes up back in Wakanda ready to lead his people with a stronger vision that includes serving other nations and bringing empowerment to those in poverty. Let us take a moment now to show the clip of my favorite part in the film.

(Show clip of T'Challa visiting with his father in the ancestral plane—similar to heaven.)

In this clip we see that T'Challa loves his father, but also challenges his father's choices on earth. T'Challa returns to earth as the Black Panther who will defeat evil through actions of compassion.

Scripture Connection

The Black Panther at multiple times in the film is a Christ-like character. Particularly toward the end of the film, when T'Challa nearly dies, only to be raised back to life, we see a humble leader who after his resurrection of sorts is able to lead with great power and compassion for others.

In our Scripture story today from John 20:1–22, we read that Mary Magdalene comes to the tomb and is heartbroken to see that the tomb is empty. She fears that someone has stolen her friend's body. As she exits the tomb, she encounters someone who appears to be a gardener. He calls her Mary and she is overjoyed with the awareness that the gardener is actually Jesus, her friend and rabbi. She seeks to embrace him and he gently directs her to go and tell the other disciples that he has risen.

Jesus then reveals himself to the disciples and calls them to live out his mission of love to the world. Similar to the Black Panther, Jesus experiences his own journey of resurrection and is empowered to lead his followers in a movement of mission to bring good news to the poor and oppressed.

There are other parallels between the *Black Panther* movie and the story of Jesus and his resurrection. Both stories explore the relationship between a father and a son. Both involve leaders with miraculous power who undergo deep suffering and death or near-death experiences. T'Challa and Jesus are prophetic leaders who guide their followers. Jesus is viewed as a king and prophet within Christianity and T'Challa is a Christ-like savior for his people and a prophet of Wakanda.

The story of the *Black Panther* especially highlights the struggles within the black community and the relationship between black people from the United States and black people from African nations. The theme of having an African nation that is technologically advanced use its power to help black people in the United States or in other underdeveloped African nations experience power and liberation is significant.

In the same way, the story of Jesus' message to his disciples to spread his message of love and resurrection is a call to the church to use our experience of the Holy Spirit to empower us to especially reach out to the vulnerable and oppressed in our communities and the world. Rather than protect our resources or look inward the church is called to sacrificially share the love of Jesus with hurting people and bring the resurrection power of the Holy Spirit as a spiritual resource, not unlike vibranium, that can help bring healing and wholeness to our communities. Will we be faithful to the mission embodied in the life of Jesus and depicted so well in the story of the *Black Panther*?

It is not a surprise to anyone that our nation continues to struggle with the problem of racism. In recent years a movement called Black Lives Matter has sparked controversy, causing political tensions that have led to protests and debates about how to address issues of poverty and injustice that more directly impact people of color. We have struggled to both support police officers while also addressing the need to improve policing so that people of color feel safe.

One of the great sorrows that fans of the *Black Panther* reflect on today is that the actor who played Black Panther, Chadwick Boseman, sadly died in 2020 of colon cancer. Boseman symbolizes both the hope of the black community and the sorrow, since he was a star in the field of acting who died too soon, not unlike other black people who hope for long, satisfying lives, but who often experience suffering and loss. Chadwick Boseman spoke of value of the movie of the *Black Panther* in an interview with CNET. Boseman shares, "This movie is about how you use power. What do you do when you get power?" he said. "The only difference between a hero and the villain is that the villain chooses to use that power in a way that is selfish and hurts other people."[9] Boseman used his power as an actor to raise awareness of the struggle of the black community and to call people to love and compassion. Boseman the actor and man has become a Christ-like figure in his own way as he now has died prematurely and lives on in the memories of those who are inspired by his example.

Another important story behind the movie *Black Panther* is of the director and cowriter of the screenplay, Ryan Coogler. In an interview with NPR, Coogler shared that when he was a boy in Oakland he went to a comic book store and asked if they had any comics with black characters. The person at the store gave him a copy of the Black Panther comic book. For Coogler, working on the *Black Panther* was partially about getting in touch with his own African roots. He explains in the interview, "This movie brought me closer to my roots. This movie took me to the continent of Africa, which is somewhere I wanted to go since my mom and dad sat me down and told me I was black, you know what I mean?"[10] Coogler successfully used the *Black Panther* movie to create a bridge between Africans and black Americans. He used the art form of film to embrace the sacred story of his own people and to inspire all people to work for peace and justice.

The movie *Black Panther* and the story of the resurrection of Jesus invite a renewed commitment to live out a missional gospel that confronts racism and understands the message of Jesus to go beyond words to include

---

9. Boseman and Trenholm, "In His Own Words."
10. Greene, "Director Ryan Coogler."

actions of love, compassion, and justice that make a difference in promoting racial reconciliation, justice, and restoration of our communities. The gospel of Jesus is the gospel of the Black Panther. Liberation of black communities and other communities of color is a key part of the mission of Jesus today. Do we understand the gospel this way or do we think of the gospel as only my personal relationship with Jesus and my personal salvation? The work of the resurrection is much greater than that, but the question is whether we will like the Black Panther and Jesus have the courage to face the injustices of the world and bring the power of love to bring about lasting change.

As I prepared this message connecting the Black Panther movie with the resurrection story of Jesus, part of me wondered how it might feel for my black sisters and brothers to hear me, a white pastor, preach on a movie that was especially highlighting the black community. Is it appropriate for me to engage this film? In the end, I am convinced that my choice to engage this movie is part of the beauty of film and Scripture. We all are to be moved by the divine transcendent whether through film or Scripture. We all are to use our voices and actions to work for justice and peace. In the end the power of the resurrection, similar to the power of vibranium, is to be resource for all to bring about equality, justice, and peace as long as we understand the necessary approach of humility and compassion. I will say that as a white man I must especially understand that my role is to listen to voices of people of color and to let them lead the effort of racial justice. I am to acknowledge my privilege and allow communities of color to show the way forward.

Please pray with me. Jesus, thank you for your word and thank you for the film *Black Panther* that help us understand your heart to bring liberation and hope to all people. Help us faithfully follow you and live out your resurrection power in our world with compassion and justice for the most vulnerable. Help us to address the problem of racism and selfishness and show us how to effectively make a difference in our town, nation, and the wider world. In the Name of Jesus we pray, AMEN.

5

Theater & Preaching

Rob O'Lynn

INTRODUCTION

Rarely am I early for anything. However, there are times that I am infuriatingly early. I will arrive early and walk on the stage. Quietly to myself, I will walk through my lines—walking on and off stage just as I will later in the evening. I rehearse my hand motions and actions, such as carrying a briefcase, sitting at a table, or—in one of my prouder moments—dying after a sword fight. The emotion is reserved; however, the intention and direction are there. I am by no means a method actor, yet this is my method of preparation. For, as Shakespeare said, the play is the thing.[1]

I have used this form of preparation for a performance for a long time. I think it goes back to my first play in high school. I was introduced to theatre much the way many church kids were in the 1990s—through puppet shows and dramatic sketches. My youth group enjoyed putting on puppet shows for the younger children in our congregation. Eventually, we would begin traveling to neighboring congregations and perform at their Vacation Bible Schools or youth worship nights. Later, we added short sketches. I would often play God (that sounds sacrilegious), the dad/teacher, or other "older" roles due to being over six feet tall and having a deep voice. And while I would enjoy this and it would lead to me founding and directing a

---

1. Shakespeare, *Hamlet* 2.2.633.

traveling Christian theatre troupe for the entirety of my college experience, it was that play during my senior year of high school that kindled a love for theatre. It was not a good play; it was what the theatre teacher could afford. It was called *Krazy Kamp*, a comedy about two summer camps—a spit-and-polish camp for girls and a chaotic camp for boys. I was cast as the director of the boys' camp and was required to recite hundreds of lines from memory while my colleague from the girls' camp read her lines off of a clipboard.

Now, I am no Tom Hanks. My first show in college was the fifteenth-century morality play *Everyman*. I played a glorified set-piece. The play was set in a modern-day parking garage, and I was one of the ensemble cast tasked with providing ambiance: I was a businessman going to a lunch, a young guy out on a date with his girlfriend, and a drifter looking for trouble. Later, I was in *Romeo and Juliet* as the Sheriff, and I also played the troupe leader that Hamlet hires to expose his father's killer. This is where I improvised a humorous death scene that is still some of my best work. My only lead part was in A. A. Milne's *The Ugly Duckling*, where I played the king . . . and forgot my lines to a crucial dialogue. Perhaps smaller roles are my forte.

Then, there was a hiatus. A fifteen-year hiatus. Honestly, it was more like an early retirement. I attended numerous productions; however, I did not pace a stage for years. And then my daughter decided to attend a theatre camp. My wife took this as an opportunity to ask me what plays would bring me out of retirement, speculating that it might be something we could do together. Oh, and by the way, our regional company is doing *To Kill a Mockingbird* (one of the plays that I had mentioned) and she booked me an audition.

(Photo credit: Bill Tussey; used with permission)

That tuned into voice-over work in *Beauty and the Beast* and *1984*, which led to me producing a couple of plays with this company. Then, I was cast last-minute as Theodore Roosevelt in the local children's troupe's production of *Newsies* (which I got to be in with my kids, both of whom are now studying theatre in college), which led me back to writing and directing sketches for my university's chapel. I am a firm believer that there are no small parts.

Yet, what does this have to do with a workbook on preaching? The easy answer is mechanics, which I will address briefly below. Even as someone living with Parkinson's disease, the "muscle memory" honed from years of performing—how I carry myself and how I speak—is still present when I preach. More than that, however, is the realization that preaching is more than giving a religious speech. Theatre helps me see the "bigger, livelier picture" of preaching, one that sees preaching as "by nature a creative event and whose purpose is to open us to God's movement."[2] Preaching is where we enter the beautifully creative theatre of salvation.

SUMMARY OF THE ART FORM

Theatre has been part of the human experience since 2500 BC in Egypt and was connected to the worship of the Greek god Dionysius as early as the sixth century BC. Although early Christianity saw theatre as "common and degenerate," the Catholic Church began allowing mystery plays (dramatizations of Bible stories), miracle plays (dramatizations of saint stories), and morality plays (dramatizations that taught moral lessons) in the medieval period.[3] One of the first recorded Christian "plays" was entitled *Quem Quaeritis* (AD tenth century), which depicts the three Marys visiting Christ's tomb.[4] These plays, along with the use of frescos and mosaics, were used to instruct a nonliterate laity yet still allowed the church to govern what was taught and how it was taught. This also led to a movement of dramatizing the Mass in the medieval period, something that remains in contemporary expressions of both Catholic and Protestant worship. However, church-based plays were banned by Pope Innocent III in 1250 and have remained largely taboo into the modern era. Yet, with the rise in popularity of theatre in Western (and, largely, American) culture, theatre in worship has once again found a welcome, if not awkward, home in the church. As Pederson notes, "One can argue that we are experiencing a true renaissance of this art form in the

---

2. Childers, *Performing the Word*, 35.
3. Chatham, *Enacting the Word*, 2.
4. Pederson, *Drama Ministry*, 13.

church. However, though drama is being accepted, most churches lack the initiative to launch, in a serious way, a drama ministry. Oftentimes drama is merely regarded as something the 'young people' do. While most church leaders could not conceive of the notion of no music in church, they think of drama as merely a nice add-on."[5] The homiletic and liturgical challenge, then, is to view theatre as another avenue through which the Spirit can draw us together for the worship of God. When used well, theatre can break down defenses and inspire meaningful worship.

Yet, why even engage in a conversation about theatre, especially in a handbook about preaching? For starters, theology and inspiration aside, there are some significant similarities between a script and Scripture. As Conrad notes in his book on one-act plays, humans are a combination of wonder and wisdom and the theatre allows us the moment to integrate these two elements of existence.[6] Play gives way to perception, such as we see with Scout in *To Kill a Mockingbird*—enjoying a moment in the summer sun only to contemplate the morality of courage the next. We see a similar concept in Scripture, as poem and parable alike kindle our imaginations regarding anthropology (a picture of humanity), theology (a picture of God), and ethic (a picture of how we should live).[7] Yet, the connection is also seen in method. Conrad tells a parable about a blind man and a deaf woman who attend a production together. The blind man, although unable to see, can hear the dialogue with its intonations and understand the play's story. And the deaf woman, although unable to hear, can see the facial expressions and physical actions and also understand the play's story.[8] In like manner, Chatham reminds us that the sermon is more than "a monologue from the pulpit."[9] It is a moment where we weave the sanctuary and the storeroom together, inviting the congregation to not only hear the sermon but also feel God working in their lives.

THEOLOGICAL AND SPIRITUAL CONNECTIONS BETWEEN PREACHING AND THEATRE

We must begin this section with the obvious elephant in the room. Is theatre not entertainment? The answer is simple: yes. Yet, as Pederson argues, "this

---

5. Pederson, *Drama Ministry*, 14.
6. Conrad, *One Act Play*, 3–4.
7. Chatham, *Enacting the Word*, 1–2.
8. Conrad, *One Act Play*, 6–7.
9. Chatham, *Enacting the Word*, 1.

fact does not need to be a negative—even in church."[10] This limited view of entertainment as applied to the arts in general—and theatre specifically—accounts for the poor reception that talk of the arts receives in the church. The church, in fact, has a "chicken and egg" paradigm. A lack of interest in theatre leads to misunderstanding the nature of drama, a lack of leadership in organization, an inability to offer and accept critique, a confusion about authenticity and integrity, and a propensity to do too much to make up for poor planning. Then the cycle begins anew. However, as Childers notes, the concern is legitimate. Yet, that does not diminish theatre's ability to point to hopeful truth and "to facilitate encounter and engender belief."[11] Despite the strained relationship between the church and the performing arts, Watts is correct when he notes that "drama . . . has become the dominant form of artistic communication in the western world."[12] And it has much to teach the preacher about their craft. When Brown talks about "inculturating the word," "embodying the word," and "animating the word," she is borrowing from the world of theatre. As she argues, "Sermon delivery is no longer a matter of 'one size fits all.'"[13] And if we believe that the preached word will "not return to [God] empty" (Isa 55:11), then *how* we deliver the sermon should be just as important as *what* we deliver.

A second connection between preaching and theatre is creativity. The opening scene of the biblical story is a scene about creativity as God creates the universe from nothing (Gen 1). In each instance, we are told that God's work was "good" (Gen 1:4, 10, 18, 21, 25). However, when it comes to the creation of humanity, God calls this work "very good" (1:31) because humanity had been created in God's image (*imago Dei*). Not only is humanity a reflection of God but humanity is also given freedom and authority to live in a responsible way that honors God.[14] This is seen in both the divine proclamation (1:28–30) and the second telling of humanity's creation (2:15–20), where there is a focus on humanity's role as co-creators (i.e., tilling the ground, naming the animals). From this scene, we can make three significant theological propositions. First, God, by choice and on purpose, creates all living things, bestowing life and fulfillment through God. Second, there is a connection between God and the world that God created, including humanity. Third, despite the finitude that God places upon creation, God still deems it "good." Thus, as we see in the writings of Tertullian and Origen, there is a

10. Pederson, *Drama Ministry*, 15.
11. Childers, *Performing the Word*, 39.
12. Watts, *Christianity and Theatre*, 8.
13. Brown, *Delivering the Sermon*, 2; see also Childers, *Performing the Word*, 57–98.
14. Brueggemann, *Genesis*, 32.

connection between God creating humanity and redeeming humanity, for humanity can only attain full creation through redemption.[15] From there on, the pages of the Bible drip with creativity, whether it is talking about architecture (Exod 25:1—31:11), music (the book of Psalms, e.g., Pss 4, 6, 43, 81, 98, 150), performance art (Ezek 4), or storytelling (Mark 4:10–12, 33–34). As McManus notes, we were created to be creative.[16] Yet, what does it mean for humanity to be creative? Are we, those created in God's image, creative as God is creative? If so, what does this mean for the nature of preaching? While thoughtful questions, they are significantly more complicated than we can answer here. Perhaps Childers's definition works best for our discussion of the spiritual connections between preaching and theatre: "Creativity may be defined simply as the bringing of something new into the world."[17] Perhaps Childers's own definition is influenced by the definition of author and playwright Marsh Cassady who once wrote that "it is catching and holding fast a fleeting moment of truth in a painting, a piece of clay, or a poem. It is discovering a new interpretation or taking something that already exists and changing it in an unpredictable way."[18] With this in mind, it is easy to argue that the homiletical work of the preacher is creative work.

Theologically speaking, the creative process may be articulated into the following three phases: *creation, incarnation,* and *transformation*.[19] In the creation phase, both preacher and performer hear the word (script) for the first time through the act of reading. Although not fully possible, the preacher attempts to empty themselves before Scripture, laboring to hear the word in its purest form. The actor first reads the script without inflection or interpretation, simply voicing the words. In both cases, this is more an act of listening than an act of reading. The next phase is incarnation, where the preacher and performer begin the process of embodying and understanding the text. Reading gives way to interpretation as ideas begin to form and arms begin to sway with the rhythm of the lines. As the preacher sits with the text and the performer sits with the script, something begins to happen. A sermon forms. A character develops. Life begins. This leads to the final phase, transformation. Here, the preacher not only develops a sermon. They become the first audience of the sermon. Change begins in the preacher as the Spirit continues its transforming work (Rom 12:1–2; Heb 4:12–13). Change occurs in the performer as they become a new character, perhaps

---

15. McGrath, *Christian Theology*, 441–42.
16. McManus, *Artisan Soul*, 4–5.
17. Childers, *Performing the Word*, 100.
18. Cassady, *Acting*, 2.
19. Childers, *Performing the Word*, 53–55.

familiar yet still different. This leads to the moment of articulation where the respective congregations are invited into the same process of creation, incarnation, and transformation as they hear the text, understand the text, and leave changed by the text. As I have noted elsewhere, preaching communicates the gospel, cultivates an encounter with God, and constructs a community of faith.[20]

INTRA-DYNAMIC ARTISTIC METHOD OF PREACHING

When thinking of methodology, Yang proposes that aesthetics is employed in three ways in preaching.[21] First, there is the illustrative approach. Here, the preacher presents an illustration to shed light on the spiritual truth being discussed. The intention is simply to illuminate an idea. In theatre, this would be what Pederson terms the "sketch" model, a six-to-eight-minute scene set in a contemporary context to provide a performed connection to the theme of the sermon.[22] The sketch, then, fronts the sermon and serves as a stand-alone element in the worship service. For example, during my college days, one of the troupe's best-known sketches was entitled "Cup of Water." The premise of the sketch was God bestowing a cup of water on a disciple and giving the instruction to use this gift in the best way possible. The action ensues when a worship leader comes by with a cough and asks for a drink, to which the disciple says they are waiting for something really important. The next scene has a youth minister miming the setup of some fireworks for a youth night. When the youth minister's hair catches on fire, they (humorously) beg for help. Thinking they cannot help, the disciple casts a few drops as the youth minister runs off stage. The final scene has a seeker come by and ask the disciple if they can talk about Jesus, to which the disciple declines. In the end, the disciple is judged for missing opportunities to demonstrate their faith by failing to show kindness or share their faith.

Second, there is the integration approach. Here, the preacher increases the significance of the aesthetic by weaving the aesthetic throughout the sermon. The intention is to connect the aesthetic to the sermon in such a way that the sermon feels incomplete without the aesthetic. In theatre, this is what Chatham terms the "guerilla theatre" model, a series of short dramatic scenes that are threaded throughout the sermon to provide an embodied texture to the sermon.[23] For a chapel sermon, I staged the narrative

20. O'Lynn, "Power of Preaching," 17.
21. Yang, *Arts and Preaching*, 85–87.
22. Pederson, *Drama Ministry*, 19–20.
23. Chatham, *Enacting the Word*, 3.

of the woman with the bleeding disorder (Mark 5:25–34) with three of my preaching students. The script was pulled from the text. The students wore their regular clothes, and the young woman who portrayed the woman in the story wore a shawl.

(Photo Credit: Rob O'Lynn)

It provided an extra level of texture to the overall service, as it was not something that we had done in some time. While this model could replace the oral reading of Scripture in the sermon, this is not really the idea. Instead, this model seeks to bring a dialogical component to the sermon where the preacher can engage in a demonstration of discipleship in the lived moment of the sermon. For example, Chatham suggests that dance could be included in a sermon from Psalm 51. As the preacher reads and preaches from the text, a dancer would embody the emotions of humility, repentance, and prostration that give way to the joy of forgiveness as the climax of the psalm.[24] In another non-theatre example, I asked two artists to paint their interpretation of Psalm 23 while I preached from the text during a chapel service. They were instructed not to talk to one another before the service. As a result, while there were some similarities in their paintings, there were also noticeable differences—which was the point of the sermon, as my focus was God being *our* shepherd.

24. Chatham, *Enacting the Word*, 69–70.

Third, there is the intra-dynamic approach. Here, the preacher further increases the significance of the aesthetic by embracing the aesthetic as the structure for the sermon. The intention is to develop the sermon in such a way that it can be "worn" (fashion), "constructed" (architecture), or "viewed" (cubism, film). In theatre, this is what Childers means by "experiencing experience," which opens us up to being vulnerable and embracing our createdness: "Theatre and preaching share the essential qualities and characteristics that can be said to be true to art in general: each probes for meaning; each is organic by nature; interest and integrity are requisite; distance plays a role; experience is the goal. In giving form to feeling, art creates something that was not there before."[25] This method does not produce a play for the sake of itself. Instead, like good theatre, this approach seeks to "encapsulate the continuing battle between order and chaos . . . even when portraying anarchy,"[26] and "is built on the chassis of change," what Yorke calls a "dramatic arc."[27]

However, we must not rush headlong into storytelling at this point, at least not traditional storytelling. It would be easy to note here the nature and function of narrative preaching. To be sure, these theories are time tested and remain highly influential.[28] Yet, the question of how effective this form of narrative preaching is with contemporary listeners continues to be debated. One of the tenets of narrative preaching—and narrative theology, from which narrative preaching is derived—is that there is a common story to which all humanity belongs: the story of God as articulated by Scripture.[29] However, what if this foundational belief is itself being questioned? Strawson is important here because he perceptively argues that not everyone agrees that this narrative arc is valid or even exists. Strawson argues that while some do adhere to a narrative arc for understanding human existence, there are some who hold to a more disjointed view of existence—what he calls "non-Narrative people."[30] Strawson further elucidates that these "non-Narrative people" are better understood as Episodic—they have no sense of narrative tying their lives together, no sense of the past from which they have come and no sense of the future to which they are going. They live only in this moment and then in the next moment and then in the next

---

25. Childers, *Performing the Word*, 37.

26. Yorke, *Into the Woods*, 77.

27. Yorke, *Into the Woods*, 90.

28. Frymire, *Preaching from Inside*, 35–41; Graves and Schlafer, *What's the Shape*, esp. 1–53.

29. Bartholomew and Goheen, *Drama of Scripture*, 19–22.

30. Strawson, "Against Narrativity," 429.

moment.[31] And while those who hold to a traditional view of narrative reality may see this perspective as empty or vapid, Strawson pushes back by saying that this is a "normal, non-pathological form of life for human beings and indeed one good form of life for human being."[32] To be sure, the loss of an overarching narrative arc has been one of the tenants of postmodernity, in terms of what it has lost from modernism.[33]

In many ways, the scene has become more important than the story. This has tremendous implications—and applications—for preaching. Building off the concerns regarding traditional narrative preaching expressed by Long,[34] Yang argues that traditional narrative preaching is losing its effectiveness and should be replaced with a more "episode-oriented" approach to preaching because narrative preaching is more chronological and "episode-oriented" preaching allows the preacher to remain contemporary.[35] As such, narrative preaching needs to go through a time of reconstruction, one that remains tied to the metanarrative of Scripture yet adopts a sense of episodic methodology. Yang points to technology writers as an example of this paradigm shift. These writers now note that cognitive fragmentation is plaguing much of society at the moment, what many refer to as being "distracted."[36] As such, it is increasingly difficult to pay attention to anything. Yet, when attention can be given, it is given momentarily. People recognize the fragmentation yet long for something meaningful to give their attention to, even if it stretches their attention span. Thus, Yang argues for the sermon to be understood as a "dramaturgical episodic plot," which consists of a hook (normal activity; inciting incident), development (initiating event; journey/crisis), climax (address), renaming and implication (resolution), denouement (restitution; putting it all together):[37]

> One crucial reason why people still like dramas is that they find, experience, and identify drama characters' life stories as their own, and reversely, enjoy imagining their own versions of life developed in dramas. . . . A drama is not simply a series of characters' short disjunctive episodes put together, but a deftly structured story with a chronological sense of the past, present,

31. Strawson, "Against Narrativity," 433.
32. Strawson, "Against Narrativity," 432–33.
33. Grenz, *Primer on Postmodernism*, 44–46.
34. Long, *Preaching from Memory*, esp. 1–26.
35. Yang, *Arts and Preaching*, 126–27.
36. Yang, *Arts and Preaching*, 128–30; see also Kalas, *Preaching in the Age of Distraction*; and Noble, *Disruptive Witness*.
37. Yang, *Arts and Preaching*, 134–37; see also Yorke, *Into the Woods*, 4–20.

and future. However, it is important to realize that people enjoy a variety of short episodes of character appearing throughout the chronological narrative, *yet at the same time they do so regardless of or with no serious concerns of the whole narrative.*[38]

The sermon, then, should demonstrate a narrative sense (dramaturgical) yet should also be rooted in the episodic moment. This tracks with Yorke's definition of a "scene": Scenes function like acts in that they "mimic an archetypal story shape."[39] Scenes have turning points because "turning points are the units of change, the key moments from a character's life."[40] Scenes can be broken down into smaller units called "beats," where comparative and contrasting motivations are revealed in a moment of dialogue.[41] And scenes progress on the moment of "action/reaction/action/reaction" until the moment of resolution.[42] To once again return to Shakespeare, the play may be the thing, however it is the scene that we pay attention to in the moment.

The question, then, is what would this "dramaturgical episodic plot" look like sermonically. This is where the proverbial rubber meets the road as we must diverge from thinking narratively and think episodically instead. The initial reaction is to think smaller than a traditional play. A traditional play, whether it be three acts or five acts, is simply too long for the sermonic context. This brings us to the one-act play. Initially, this looks promising, as one-act plays are generally twenty-five to thirty minutes long (forty-five minutes at the most). Although not as widely popular as full stage plays or musicals, Yorke reminds us that "one act plays can be traced back as far as Euripides' *Cyclops*," which was loosely based on the epic of Odysseus and was first staged in the fifth century BC.[43] Conrad's formula for a one-act play follows the same scaffolding as a traditional play—Normal Activity (establishes context), Initiating Event (the problem), Address (attempts to solve the problem), Resolution (successful solution), Restitution (the payoff).[44] However, a one-act play follows Aristotle's three "unities" for playwriting—time (all plays take place in a moment of time), place (all plays take place somewhere), and action (all plays do something)—more closely than longer plays because the goal of a one-act play is "to see if your characters can

---

38. Yang, *Arts and Preaching*, 136 (emphasis original).
39. Yorke, *Into the Woods*, 91.
40. Yorke, *Into the Woods*, 91.
41. Yorke, *Into the Woods*, 93.
42. Yorke, *Into the Woods*, 94.
43. Yorke, *Into the Woods*, 25.
44. Conrad, *One Act Play*, 16.

effectively tell a story" in a shorter period.⁴⁵ I mentioned earlier that I was in a production of Milne's *The Ugly Duckling* in college. In the play, a king (me) attempts to arrange the marriage of his daughter to the prince of a rival kingdom. He concocts a scheme to palm his daughter's handmaid off as his daughter while, unknowingly, the prince conspires similarly with his servant. Naturally, hilarity ensues as the two servants fall in love and the prince and princess also fall in love without the trappings of royalty—all within about forty-five minutes! The action is quick and the dialogue rattles off of the tongue. However, there are six characters total and, eventually, eight storylines occurring all at the same time (insert shocked emoji here)!

Following Yang's concern about the episodic experience, not only is the traditional play not an option of this "dramaturgical episodic plot," but neither is the traditional one-act. There is simply too much plot, too many characters, and too much dialogue. Perhaps the one-performer show may serve as an option? In 2019, my family and I traveled to New York City for a week of taking in shows. We saw *Mean Girls: The Musical*, *Be More Chill*, and *Hadestown* (which I *highly* recommend). We also saw *Sea Wall/A Life*, starring Tom Sturridge and Jake Gyllenhaal. In this two-act, two-man show, each actor performed a monologue that *Variety* referred to as "devastating" and "heartbreaking," as each dialogue reflects on love, death, and grief.⁴⁶

(Photo Credit: Rob O'Lynn)

45. Conrad, *One Act Play*, 2.
46. Stasio, "Broadway Review."

The sets were bare and the monologues sharply were emotional. In many ways, these individual acts each represented the best of what narrative preaching attempts. The problem is that there is still a lot of story to churn through in these types of performances. Although these productions are performed by only a single actor, each play still comprised a handful of scenes.

With that in mind, perhaps we can turn to the monologue, especially since we are considering the sermon as a homiletical "scene" rather than a full performance. A monologue, according to Spencer, is a "direct address to the audience" where an actor articulates their "internal thoughts," revealing emotion or intention that may not be readily evident to the other characters or even the audience but provides significant context to the plot.[47] The most famous monologue is Hamlet's "To be or not to be" soliloquy (3.1.56–89). Shakespeare was the master of the soliloquy because it provided the opportunity for the stage crew to reset the stage while major characters kept the story going with an extended speech.[48] However, only Shakespeare really used soliloquies. Eugene O'Neill, on the other hand, developed what Spencer calls the "seamless monologue," where a character turns to another character onstage and advances the plot through an extended monologue—such as Edmond does to Tyrone in *Long Day's Journey into Night*.[49] Examples of this type of monologue include Willy's monologue about Dave Singleman from Arthur Miller's *Death of a Salesman*, Troy Maxson's emotional self-reflective monologue from August Wilson's *Fences*, or Georgina's mourning monologue from Elmer Rice's *Dream Girl*. The speeches drip with emotion and require little narrative arc to connect with the audience, unless the audience is unfamiliar with the larger play.

Before going any further, I need to offer a warning—you need to buckle up for what is coming next. The "dramaturgical episodic plot" is unlike any kind of sermon crafting that we have ever considered. To be sure, there is a real concern here. Reducing a sermon to a single scene or monologue runs the risk of the sermon suffering from "plotlessness," a stringing together of unconnected movements that demonstrate no cause-and-effect.[50] While this might work for Strawson in a meta sense, if we believe anything about preaching, it is that preaching should say something. Therefore, we will think of crafting a "dramaturgical episodic plot" sermon in terms of structure and movement. In terms of structure, the "dramaturgical episodic plot" sermon will find unity in Aristotle's concepts of time, place, and action. Exegetically

---

47. Spencer, *Playwright's Guidebook*, 66.
48. Jeffreys, *Playwriting*, 58.
49. Spencer, *Playwright's Guidebook*, 259.
50. Spencer, *Playwright's Guidebook*, 212.

speaking, this means that the text for the sermon will remain with a simple pericope of scripture. For example, the pericope could be the story of Jesus' encounter with Zacchaeus (Luke 19:1–10). It could be the scene itself as articulated in Scripture or it could be a dramatic recounting framed later in Zacchaeus's life. However, the time is confined to the time period of Luke 19, the place is confined to Jericho, and the action is confined to the singular conversation between Jesus and Zacchaeus. Ultimately, we are crafting what Truby calls a "ministry," an entire story that introduces the character, defines the conflict, reveals the strategy that satiates the desire, and provides resolution without a single wipe.[51]

Then, following Yang's plot outline mentioned above, the monological scene follows the pattern of hook, development, climax, renaming and implication, and denouement. We may also phrase the beats as questions:

- Hook—What happened?
- Development—Why did it happen?
- Climax—What resolution is offered?
- Renaming and implication—How do I connect?
- Denouement—Is an invitation accepted?

In the example of Jesus' encounter with Zacchaeus, the plot would follow like this: Jesus enters into a town to find a tax collector who wants to see him; however, he is unable to do so (hook). This happens because he is short in stature and unable to see Jesus over the crowds, but also because his position has ostracized him from the Jewish community (development). Sensing the desire to find him, Jesus stops and invites Zacchaeus into his presence so that he may experience an invitation to salvation (climax). Those listening to this sermon, hopefully, will sense their connection to Zacchaeus, as they have encountered Christ through the sermon (renaming and implication). The claim made by Jesus, that he can offer salvation to anyone who comes to him, is considered by the episodic listener and a step toward reintegrating into the larger arc of God's story is taken (denouement). Much of this indeed reflects more storytelling-oriented forms of preaching. However, this differs in two major ways: First, there is a stark awareness that those listening have no awareness of and hold no allegiance to the story of Scripture, thus all the trappings of backstory and narrative arc are left in the minister's study. Second, with these trappings removed, the freshness of the individual encounter can be highlighted. The episodic listener is more like Zacchaeus than they realize and can encounter Jesus similarly.

51. Truby, *Anatomy of Story*, 373–75.

SERMON PLANNING WORKSHEET[52]

Text: [*a singular text that is a complete unit of thought*]

Analysis of Text: [*Analysis should demonstrate careful attention to language, rhetoric, and theology of the text, as well as engagement with passage beyond a casual reading (i.e., commentary work). The analysis should also consider Aristotle's concepts of time, place, and action.*]

Theme: [*complete sentence of five to seven words that encapsulates the idea of the sermon, as drawn from the text*]

Doctrine: [*declares a recognized concept of Christian theology; can be either a systematic concept or a spiritual concept*]

Need: [*declares a recognized concern from the text or a recognized contemporary need that connects directly to the text*]

Image: [*either a single image or collection of images that connect directly to the theme*]

Mission: [*provides an application that is* concrete, object-driven, *and* measurable, *as well as provides a strategy or an example*[53]]

Moving from Text to Sermon:

- Hook—What happened?
- Development—Why did it happen?
- Climax—What resolution is offered?
- Renaming and implication—How do I connect?
- Denouement—Is an invitation accepted?

SAMPLE SERMON: "NEITHER DO I"

- **Text:** John 7:53—8:11
- **Textual Analysis:** This passage, also known as the *Pericope Adulterae*, is often debated for its validity in the canon based on its textual placement, as many scholars find it out of sync with the theology and rhetoric of the Fourth Gospel. For example, Metzger has noted that the passage contains vocabulary and a writing style different from

---

52. Here I am following Wilson's concept of "sermon unity": *Four Pages*, 41–57.

53. For more on this idea, see O'Lynn, "Crafting Sermon Applications."

the remainder of the Gospel and contains an interruption in narrative flow from 7:52 to 8:12, where Jesus moves from inside the temple to outside the temple to back inside the temple without physically moving.[54] Additionally, this is the only place where scribes and elders are mentioned in the Fourth Gospel. Historically, this passage did not appear in Johannine manuscripts until after AD 900, although it was known to leading church fathers like Jerome, Ambrose, and Augustine, as well as Papias (one of John's disciples).[55] That being said, how Jesus functions in the passage is certainly consistent with his actions in other passages in the Gospel (i.e., cleansing the temple in 2:13–25, speaking with the Samaritan woman in 4:1–42, or challenging unbelief in him in 12:36–43). Both in his rhetorical response about only those without sin casting the first stone and the theological implication that this response holds as the woman still expects Jesus to condemn her, Jesus counters the trap, for "power, not righteousness, was their major concern,"[56] and demonstrates the mercy of redemption.

- **Theme:** Jesus provides redemption. A sermon from this text will consider the fixed time and location of the passage and will be framed from the perspective of the disciple John.
- **Doctrine:** Salvation.
- **Need:** Any sin can be forgiven, if given to Jesus.
- **Image:** Imagery provided by text.
- **Mission:** To respond to Jesus' invitation for salvation and discipleship.

Sermon Script

Have you ever seen something that just took your breath away, that stopped you cold in your tracks, and caused you to pause for a moment? Maybe you came across an accident on the highway or witnessed someone being cruel to someone else. Or maybe you witnessed a beautiful sunrise or came across a child being kind to a friend. In that moment, whether good or bad, you are frozen in time, unable to move or react. You do not know what to do until something—an action of another or something said—snaps you back into reality. Then, you find your footing again and are able to move out of or appreciate the moment you are in. There are a lot of moments in my life

---

54. Metzger, *Textual Commentary*, 187–90.
55. Holmes, *Apostolic Fathers in English*, 304.
56. McLarty, *Journey of Faith*, 147.

that would count for something like this. However, there is this one moment that often comes to mind.

It has been awhile now since that strange afternoon; however, the events of what happened are still crystal clear. It was a day spent with my teacher. Those days were great because it seemed like something interesting always happened. I had been studying under this teacher for about three years and every lesson pushed me and challenged me in ways that I could not have imagined. Then there would be times that he would test us by asking us to demonstrate what we had learned by teaching others or helping others. I always wanted to do well, yet I would often find myself coming up short. However, he would smile, tell me it was okay, and move on. Then, there was this day. It was during one of our religious festivals—I mean one of the big ones. My teacher had spent most of the day teaching in the temple. Or was it out in the market? Anyways, he was in mid-sentence about showing compassion to our enemies when a group of religious leaders smashed through the crowd that had gathered around my teacher. They threw a woman down at his feet and shouted something about how she had been caught having an affair with another man and these men wanted my teacher to judge her for them.

This is when time froze in this moment. My teacher did not finish his sentence. He simply lowered his hand and looked down at the woman who had been thrown at his feet. The gaze of everyone in the crowd followed. The woman was something of a mystery. It was clear that she was beautiful, with lovely, long hair and a glistening complexion. I imagined that I had seen her in the marketplace. However, she was not working in one of the shops or selling fruit at one of the produce stalls. She had shopped at the market; I was sure of it! I remembered her long, flowing purple robe lined with gold stitching. Her shawl had covered most of her face; however, her eyes had caught mine and betrayed my stare with a smile. I do not know why, but I was embarrassed when she saw me. Did she see me? Now, however, this woman was laying on the ground in a heap, sobbing and tattered, with only a sheet draped around her as blood trickled from her knees where she had fallen. She was not just broken; she was shattered.

"What do you say" (John 8:5)?!

I—and everyone else—snapped back to reality with the question. While I was lost in thought, I had missed the accusation that revealed why this woman was laying before us shattered and bleeding. The religious leaders had caught her having an affair with a man that she was not married to—a serious crime in our culture. Our law was quite clear on this matter. There had to be at least two witnesses with corroborating testimony about the legal infraction. In this case, at least two people had to have visual proof of the affair—of the persons involved, where the affair was happening, things like that. This may seem brazen to you, maybe even voyeuristic. However, our laws demand that we maintain communal purity. If one person breaks the law, it is up to the community to govern for restoration. However, in this case, the law called for a severe punishment—stoning. Yet, it was a stoning of both individuals. And where is the man that she was having the affair with?

Questions were filling my mind. I looked over at my teacher for guidance; however, his direction was still pointed down. Yet, he was not looking at the woman. No, instead he was crouched down to the ground and was writing something in the sand. Was it names? Words? I could not tell. I asked him about it later and he simply gave me that smile that he would give when I had tried to do something that he had taught me and watched me come up a bit short. After a few moments, he looked at the woman for only a moment. But in that moment, he looked deep into her soul it seemed. He rose and calmly said to all who could hear, "Let anyone among you who is without sin be the first to throw a stone at her" (John 8:8). The cheering and jeering that I had blocked out rushed back into my ears in an instant, so much so it almost knocked me down. Then, in the next instant there was a sharp silence, drummed over only with the sound of stones falling to the ground. The shuffle of feet came next as those who had gathered left. Even I and my fellow students left, weighed down with our own guilt that we had become unexpectedly aware of.

Although I walked away, I could still hear what my teacher said to the woman who lay shattered and bleeding at his feet. He asked her if anyone remained to accuse her of her crime. She braved to look around the part of the sheet that was covering her face and saw only my teacher. She responded that no one else was left to accuse her. Then he crouched back down, looked her right in the eye, smiled and said, "Neither do I condemn you. Go your way, and from now on do not sin again" (John 8:11). Then, he helped her up and called for us to help her home while he returned to teaching. I had heard my teacher talk about mercy countless times. Yet, on that day, I saw what mercy looks like. I experienced it for the first time. I finally understood what the law had talked about when it mentioned redemption, to be cleansed of guilt and to live a new kind of life.

I appreciate you coming to hear my story, I really do. I love to talk about my teacher—his name is Jesus, by the way. He radically changed my life for the good. Although I have not always understood what he said or did—I still do not—I have always tried to share what he did for me. I thought I knew how to live rightly by following the law. I thought I knew what not living rightly looked like. However, my understanding was immature until I met my teacher, until I met Jesus. He showed me what mercy, redemption, peace, hope, joy, and love—oh, what beautiful love—really looked like. You may think that you have it all figured out. I say this with all the kindness I can—you do not unless you are following the teacher, and, even then, it will take time to figure out. My teacher did not come to condemn but to forgive, an offer that he still makes today.

Epilogue

As I sit to pen this epilogue, the echoes of our first Zoom meeting reverberate with a clarity that belies the year's progression. It was a meeting defined by eagerness and a shared vision, where the flickering screens could not diminish the vibrant enthusiasm that leapt from each participant. A year on, this vibrancy has only intensified, as if the countless hours spent in contemplation, discussion, and creation have imbued our collective spirit with a profound sense of purpose.

Our gatherings were few, but the depth of our connection belied the brevity of our encounters. Twice we met through the portals of technology, and twice we stood together under Oregon's expansive skies, our minds and hearts converging in pursuit of a single goal: to transform preaching through the lens of art, to make it resonate with the aesthetic yearnings of our time.

We gathered not as mere colleagues, but as artisans of the word, each of us sculpting sermons that aspired to touch souls as deftly as a painter's brush calls forth emotions from a blank canvas. Our meeting spaces—hotel lobbies, quaint restaurants, and the familiar nooks of coffee shops—became our studios. Here, amid the clatter of cups and the low hum of conversations, our project found its pulse.

The delight was palpable, an undercurrent in every exchange. A shared vision had united us, a belief in the profound purpose of our work, as articulated in the prologue. This was not merely a task; it was a calling, a shared commitment to infuse the sacred art of preaching with the vibrant energy of the arts.

Over the span of our project, a transformation unfolded within us. Our preaching, once confined to the constraints of tradition, began to adopt the hues and textures of our artistic exploration. Sermons took flight, buoyed by the creativity that had been stirred in our workshops. Some of us ventured to put our theories to the test, crafting homilies that drew directly from the chapters we penned. The feedback was as diverse as the audience itself. For some, it was a revelation, a sermon that could be seen, felt, tasted, and touched—a sensory embodiment of the word. For others, it was a step on a longer journey, one that required refinement, further exploration. Yet, the overwhelming consensus was clear: this approach was not just viable; it was vital.

This endeavor reaffirmed a timeless lesson, akin to the foundational teachings of Preaching 101: the journey toward eloquent sermonizing is eternal. Like artists before a canvas, preachers are called to reflect, to practice, to evolve ceaselessly. Perfection in preaching, as in art, is a horizon always receding, always compelling us to reach beyond our grasp. Our handbook, then, is not just a repository of knowledge but a testament to the art of continual transformation.

Yet, as we bid farewell, a note of collective "regret" emerged. Our exploration had delved into only five art forms, while the vast expanse of human creativity stretches far beyond our scope. Therefore, we earnestly hope to continue this initial journey, embracing a wide, open-ended future. We are considering the possibility of a second or third volume that would explore the intersectional possibilities of various other art forms with preaching.

Bibliography

BOOKS

Allen, Ronald. *Contemporary Biblical Interpretation*. Valley Forge, PA: Judson, 2009.
———, ed. *Patterns of Preaching: A Sermon Sampler*. St. Louis: Chalice, 2004.
Augustine. *Treatises on Marriage and Other Subjects*. Translated by Charles T. Wilcox et al. Washington, DC: Catholic University of America Press, 1999.
Barth, Karl. *The Christian Life: Church Dogmatics IV/4, Lecture Fragments*. Translated by Geoffrey W. Bromiley. Grand Rapids: Eerdmans, 1981.
Bartholomew, Craig G., and Michael W. Goheen. *The Drama of Scripture: Finding Our Place in the Biblical Story*. 2nd ed. Grand Rapids: Baker Academic, 2014.
Beasley-Murray, George Raymond. *John*. Waco, TX: Word, 1987.
Bernier, Jonathan. *Aposynagōgos and the Historical Jesus in John: Rethinking the Historicity of the Johannine Expulsion Passages*. Leiden: Brill, 2013.
Bolton, Andrew. *Alexander McQueen: Savage Beauty*. New York: Metropolitan Museum of Art, 2011.
Bondi, Roberta C. *To Pray and to Love: Conversations on Prayer with the Early Church*. Minneapolis: Fortress, 1991.
Boston, Thomas. *Human Nature in Its Four-Fold State: Of Primitive Integrity, Entire Depravity, Begun Recovery, and Consummate Happiness or Misery*. London: J. Chalmers, 1793.
Bratt, James D., ed. *Abraham Kuyper: A Centennial Reader*. Grand Rapids: Eerdmans, 1998.
Brown, Teresa L. Fry. *Delivering the Sermon*. Elements of Preaching Series. Minneapolis: Fortress, 2008.
Brueggemann, Walter. *Genesis*. Interpretation: A Bible Commentary for Teaching and Preaching. Atlanta: Westminster John Knox, 1982.
Cargal, Timothy B. *Hearing a Film, Seeing a Sermon: Preaching and Popular Movies*. Louisville: Westminster John Knox, 2007.
Cassady, Marsh. *Acting, Step by Step*. San Jose, CA: Resource Publications, 1988.
Chatham, James O. *Enacting the Word: Using Drama in Preaching*. Louisville: Westminster John Knox, 2002.
Childers, Jana. *Performing the Word: Preaching as Theatre*. Nashville: Abingdon, 1998.

Bibliography

Choi, Young-Sil. *Women in the New Testament*. Seoul: Dongyeon, 2012.
Conrad, Reid. *The One Act Play: An Introduction to Playwriting*. Independently published, 2020.
Craddock, Fred B. *As One Without Authority: Revised and with New Sermons*. St. Louis: Chalice, 2001.
———. *Overhearing the Gospel*. St. Louis: Chalice, 2002.
Frymire, Jeffrey W. *Preaching from Inside the Story: A Fresh Journey into Narrative*. Lloyd John Ogilvie Institute of Preaching Series. Eugene, OR: Cascade, 2022.
Fujimura, Makoto. *Art and Faith: A Theology of Making*. New Haven, CT: Yale University Press, 2020.
Gench, Frances Taylor. *Back to the Well: Women's Encounters with Jesus in the Gospels*. Louisville: Westminster John Knox, 2004.
Graves, Mike, and David J. Schlafer, eds. *What's the Shape of Narrative Preaching? Essays in Honor of Eugene L. Lowry*. St. Louis: Chalice, 2008.
Grayzel, Solomon. *The Church and the Jews in the Thirteenth Century*. 2nd ed. New York: Hermon Press, 1966.
Grenz, Stanley J. *A Primer on Postmodernism*. Grand Rapids: Eerdmans, 1996.
Han, Mi-ra. *When Women Read the Bible*. Seoul: Christian Literature Society of Korea, 2002.
Holmes, Michael W. *The Apostolic Fathers in English*. Grand Rapids: Baker Academic, 2006.
Jeffreys, Stephen. *Playwriting: Structure, Character, How, and What to Write*. Edited by Maeve McKeown. New York: Theatre Communications Group, 2019.
Johnston, Robert K. *Reel Spirituality: Theology and Film in Dialogue*. 2nd ed. Grand Rapids: Baker Academic, 2006.
Kalas, J. Ellsworth. *Preaching in an Age of Distraction*. Downers Grove, IL: InterVarsity, 2014.
Kim, Jean Kyoung. *Woman and Nation: An Intercontextual Reading of the Gospel of John from a Postcolonial Feminist Perspective*. Boston: Brill, 2004.
Klink, Edward W., III. *The Sheep of the Fold: The Audience and Origin of the Gospel of John*. Cambridge: Cambridge University Press, 2007.
Long, Thomas G. *Preaching from Memory to Hope*. Louisville: Westminster John Knox, 2009.
———. *The Witness of Preaching*. Louisville: Westminster John Knox, 2005.
Lowry, Eugene L. *The Homiletical Plot: The Sermon as Narrative Art Form*. Louisville: Westminster John Knox, 2000.
McGrath, Alister E. *Christian Theology: An Introduction*. 3rd ed. Malden, MA: Blackwell, 2001.
McKenzie, Alyce M. *Making a Scene in the Pulpit: Vivid Preaching for Visual Listeners*. Louisville: Westminster John Knox, 2018.
McLarty, Bruce. *Journey of Faith: Walking with Jesus Through the Gospel of John*. Searcy, AR: Resource, 1997.
McManus, Erwin Raphael. *The Artisan Soul: Crafting Your Life into a Work of Art*. New York: HarperOne, 2014.
McNamara, Denis R. *Catholic Church Architecture and the Spirit of the Liturgy*. Chicago: Hillenbrand, 2009.
Merleau-Ponty, Maurice. *Phenomenology of Perception*. Translated by Donald A. Landes. London: Routledge, 2012.

Metzger, Bruce. *A Textual Commentary on the Greek New Testament.* 2nd ed. Stuttgart: German Bible Society, 1994.
Mitchell, Nathan D. *Meeting Mystery: Liturgy, Worship, Sacraments.* New York: Orbis, 2006.
Noble, Alan. *Disruptive Witness: Speaking Truth in a Distracted Age.* Downers Grove, IL: InterVarsity, 2018.
Otto, Rudolf. *The Idea of the Holy: An Inquiry into the Non-Rational Factor in the Idea of the Divine and Its Relation to the Rational.* Translated by John W. Harvey. New York: Oxford University Press, 1958.
Pastoureau, Michel. *Blue: The History of a Color.* Princeton: Princeton University Press, 2023.
Pederson, Steve. *Drama Ministry: Practical Help for Making Drama a Vital Part of Your Church.* Grand Rapids: Zondervan, 1999.
Phillips, John. *Exploring Genesis: An Expository Commentary.* Grand Rapids: Kregel Academic, 2001.
Schneiders, Sandra Marie. *The Revelatory Text: Interpreting the New Testament as Sacred Scripture.* 2nd ed. Collegeville, MN: Liturgical, 1999.
Schottroff, Luise. *Lydia's Impatient Sisters: A Feminist Social History of Early Christianity.* Louisville: Westminster John Knox, 1995.
Spencer, Stuart. *The Playwright's Guidebook: An Insightful Primer on the Art of Dramatic Writing.* New York: Farrar, Straus and Giroux, 2002.
Swartley, Willard M. *John.* Harrisonburg, VA: Herald, 2013.
Tertullian. "On the Apparel of Women." In *Ante-Nicene Fathers*, edited by A. Cleveland Coxe et al., 4:14–25. Peabody, MA: Hendrickson, 1995.
Truby, John. *The Anatomy of Story: 22 Steps to Becoming a Master Storyteller.* New York: Farrar, Straus and Giroux, 2007.
Watts, Murray. *Christianity and Theatre.* Edinburgh: Handsel, 1986.
Wilson, Paul Scott. *The Four Pages of the Sermon: A Guide to Biblical Preaching.* Rev. ed. Nashville: Abingdon, 2018.
Winner, Lauren F. *Wearing God: Clothing, Laughter, Fire, and Other Overlooked Ways of Meeting God.* New York: HarperOne, 2015.
Woodley, Randy S. *Indigenous Theology and the Western Worldview: A Decolonized Approach to Christian Doctrine.* Grand Rapids: Baker Academic, 2022.
Yang, Sunggu A. *Arts and Preaching: An Aesthetic Homiletic for the Twenty-First Century.* Eugene, OR: Cascade, 2021.
Yorke, John. *Into the Woods: How Stories Work and Why We Tell Them.* New York: Penguin, 2013.

BOOK CHAPTERS, ARTICLES, AND LECTURES

Boseman, Chadwick, and Richard Trenholm. "In His Own Words: Chadwick Boseman on What Black Panther Meant to Him." CNET, Sept. 2, 2020. https://www.cnet.com/culture/entertainment/chadwick-boseman-what-black-panther-meant-to-him-2017-interview/.
Covolo, Robert S. "Re-Fashioning Faith: The Promise of a Kuyperian Theology of Fashion." *Cultural Encounters* 5:2 (2009) 41–62.

"Cyber Violence Against Women." European Institute for Gender Equality. https://eige.europa.eu/gender-based-violence/cyber-violence-against-women.

Deans, Thomas. "The Rhetoric of Jesus Writing in the Story of the Woman Accused of Adultery (John 7.53–8.1)." *College Composition and Communication* 65:3 (2014) 406–29.

Galloni, Alessandra. "Prada vs. Prada: Overcoming Fashion Phobia." *Wall Street Journal*, Feb. 17, 2007. https://www.wsj.com/articles/SB116907782780879498.

Gench, Frances Taylor. "John 7:53—8:11." *Interpretation (Richmond)* 63:4 (2009) 398–400.

Greene, David. "Director Ryan Coogler Says 'Black Panther' Brought Him Closer to His Roots." NPR, Feb. 15, 2018. https://www.npr.org/2018/02/15/585702642/director-ryan-coogler-says-black-panther-brought-him-closer-to-his-roots.

Guardiola-Sáenz, Leticia. "Border-Crossing and Its Redemptive Power in John 7.53—8.11: A Cultural Reading of Jesus and the Accused." In *John and Postcolonialism: Travel, Space and Power*, edited by Musa W. Dube and Jeffrey L. Staley, 129–52. New York: Sheffield Academic Press/Continuum, 2002.

Handayani, Dwi Maria. "Does God Care About Fashion?" *Missiology: An International Review* 49:3 (2021) 300–9.

Harvie, Timothy. "Political Lament: Extinction, Grief, and Embodied Silence." *Studies in Religion/Sciences Religieuses* 50:3 (2021) 419–29.

Horsley, Richard A. "Synagogues in Galilee and the Gospels." In *Evolution of the Synagogue: Problems and Progress*, edited by Howard. C. Kee and Lynn H. Cohick, 46–69. Harrisburg: Trinity Press International, 1999.

Hurtado, Leonardo. "Autumn/Winter 1995: Season Coverage." https://archived.co/Alexander-McQueen-Autumn-Winter-1995 (link no longer active).

Joplin, Patricia Klindienst. "Intolerable Language: Jesus and the Woman Taken in Adultery." In *Shadow of Spirit: Postmodernism and Religion*, edited by Philippa Berry and Andrew Wernick, 226–37. London: Routledge, 1992.

Kang, Pil. "Comforting All the Parents in the World Who Have Lost Their Children: The Love of Käthe Kollwitz." In *Painters' Life Paintings: Moments of Wounding and Healing in Self-Portraiture*, 246–60. Seoul: Knowledge, 2022.

Kinukawa, Hisako. "On John 7:53—8:11: A Well-Cherished but Much-Clouded Story." In *Reading from This Place: Social Location and Biblical Interpretation in Global Perspective*, edited by Fernando F. Segovia and Mary Ann Tolbert, 2:82–96. Minneapolis: Fortress, 1995.

Klein, Alyssa Vingan. "Marc Jacobs' Spare, Silent Runway Show Made the Loudest Impact of Fashion Week." *Fashionista*, Feb. 16, 2017. https://fashionista.com/2017/02/marc-jacobs-fall-2017-review.

Louw, D. J. "Preaching as Art (Imaging the Unseen) and Art as Homiletics (Verbalising the Unseen): Towards the Aesthetics of Iconic Thinking and Poetic Communication in Homiletics." *HTS Teologiese Studies/Theological Studies* 72:2 (2016) a3826. https://doi.org/10.4102/hts.v72i2.3826.

Manus, C. U., and J. C. Ukaga. "The Narrative of the Woman Caught in Adultery (Jn 7:53—8:1–11) Reread in the Nigerian Context." *Acta Theologica* 37:1 (2017) 56–85.

McCaulley, Esau. "How Are We as the Church Trying to Shape the Christian Imagination?" Lecture, Nov. 28, 2023. Life Change Church, Portland, OR.

Mudimeli, L. M., and J. van der Westhuizen. "Unheard Voices of Women in the Bible, with Implication of Empowerment in the Context of Today's Church." *Acta Theologica, Supplementum* 27 (2019) 118–31.

O'Connor, Kathleen. "Voices Arguing About Meaning." In *Lamentations in Ancient and Contemporary Cultural Context*, edited by Nancy Lee and Carleen Mandolfo, 27–31. Atlanta: SBL, 2008.

O'Day, Gail R. "Gospel of John." In *Women's Bible Commentary*, edited by Carol A. Newsom and Sharon H. Ringe, 517–31. 3rd ed. Louisville: Westminster John Knox, 2012.

———. "John 7:53—8:11: A Study in Misreading." *Journal of Biblical Literature* 111 (1992) 631–40.

O'Lynn, Rob. "Crafting Sermon Applications That Stick." Preaching Today. https://www.preachingtoday.com/preaching-guides/sermon-application/crafting-sermon-applications-that-stick.html.

———. "The Power of Preaching." *The Lookout* 7 (June 23, 2019) 16–17.

O'Sullivan, Michael. "Reading John 7:53—8:11 as a Narrative Against Male Violence Against Women." *Hervormde Teologiese Studies* 71:1 (2015) 1–8.

Park, Rohun. "Revisiting the Parable of the Prodigal Son for Decolonization: Luke's Reconfiguration of Oikos in 15:11–32." *Biblical Interpretation* 17:5 (2009) 507–20.

Porter, Josh. "Why Did Jesus Speak in Parables?" BibleProject, Jan. 27, 2020. https://bibleproject.com/articles/are-the-parables-of-jesus-confusing-on-purpose/.

Rabie-Boshof, Annelien. "The Pericope Adulterae (John 7:53—8:11): Jesus' Answer, an Offer of Life to Suffering Women." *Perichoresis* 19:4 (2021) 3–20.

Stasio, Marilyn. "Broadway Review: Jake Gyllenhaal in 'Sea Wall/A Life.'" *Variety*, Aug. 8, 2019. https://variety.com/2019/legit/reviews/sea-wall-a-life-review-jake-gyllenhaal-broadway-1203292445/.

Strawson, Galen. "Against Narrativity." *Ratio* n.s. 17:4 (Dec. 2004) 428–52.

Sullivan, Louis H. "Tall Office Building Artistically Considered." *Lippincott's Magazine*, March 1896, 403–9.

Thistlethwaite, Susan Brooks. "Every Two Minutes: Battered Women and Feminist Interpretation." In *Feminist Interpretation of the Bible*, edited by Letty M. Russell, 96–107. Philadelphia: Westminster, 1985.

Thoufeekh, Shairah. "Marc Jacobs Fall 2017." *L'Officiel Singapore*, Feb. 21, 2017. https://www.lofficielsingapore.com/fashion/marc-jacobs-fall-2017-ready-to-wear-runway-collection-pictures-new-york-fashion-week.

Toensing, Holly J. "Divine Intervention or Divine Intrusion? Jesus and the Adulterer in John's Gospel." In *A Feminist Companion to John*, edited by Amy-Jill Levine and Marianne Blickenstaff, 1:159–72. London: Sheffield Academic, 2002.

Weren, Wim J. C. "The Use of Violence in Punishing Adultery in Biblical Texts (Deuteronomy 22:13–29 and John 7:53—8:11)." In *Coping with Violence in the New Testament*, edited by Pieter G. R. de Villiers and Jan Willem van Henten, 133–50. Leiden: Brill, 2012.

Young, Yi Mi. "Two Anonymous Women Who Created a Theological Space with Questions and Silence." *The Journal of Pastoral Care and Counseling* 39 (2022) 41–73.

MEDIA SOURCES

"All About Cubism." Tate, 2023. https://www.tate.org.uk/art/art-terms/c/cubism/all-about-cubism.

Bibliography

"Altar Window (FUMC Stain Glass Window Series)." First United Methodist Church of Santa Rosa, June 5, 2023. YouTube video. https://www.youtube.com/watch?v=LB7__s92Y9w.

Cameron, James, dir. *Titanic*. Los Angeles: Paramount Pictures, 2007. DVD.

"Clerestory Window (FUMC Stain Glass Window Series)." First United Methodist Church of Santa Rosa, July 26, 2023. YouTube video. https://www.youtube.com/watch?v=RygVDs2D-2o.

"The History of Cubism: From Pablo Picasso to Georges Braque." unschooled_art, Feb. 21, 2023. YouTube video. https://www.youtube.com/watch?v=HZO__bc0Pio.

Mackie, Tim, and Jon Collins. "Decoding the Parables." *BibleProject Podcast*, Apr. 13, 2020. https://bibleproject.com/podcast/decoding-parables/.

Murphy, Michael. "Architecture That's Built to Heal." TED, Oct. 6, 2026. https://www.youtube.com/watch?v=MvXZzKZ3JYQ.

Roberts Architecture, "What Is Architecture?" YouTube video. Apr. 10, 2023. https://youtu.be/tfN5sgQjSiI.

"Round Window (FUMC Stain Glass Window Series)." First United Methodist Church of Santa Rosa, June 15, 2023. YouTube video. https://www.youtube.com/watch?v=pJWyJxDUT2o.

"Runway Fall 2017 Marc Jacobs." Marc Jacobs, Feb. 16, 2017. YouTube video. https://www.youtube.com/watch?v=4rLg2wsC1SU.

www.ingramcontent.com/pod-product-compliance
Lightning Source LLC
Chambersburg PA
CBHW071007160426
43193CB00012B/1949